DISCOVERY PROBLEMS IN CIVIL CASES

By Joseph L. Ebersole and Barlow Burke

Federal Judicial Center
April, 1980

This publication is a product of a study undertaken in furtherance of the Center's statutory mission to conduct and stimulate research and development on matters of judicial administration. The analyses, conclusions, and points of view are those of the authors. This work has been subjected to staff review within the Center, and publication signifies that it is regarded as responsible and valuable. It should be emphasized, however, that on matters of policy the Center speaks only through its Board.

FJC-R-80-3

TABLE OF CONTENTS

I. INTRODUCTION 1

II. THE SURVEY 4

    Methodology 4
    Survey Results 5

III. DISCOVERY PROBLEMS PERCEIVED BY REPORTING ATTORNEYS 10

    Resistance to Discovery 11
        General Resistance 11
        Assertion of a Privilege 12
        Resisting Document Production 13
        Resisting Answers to Interrogatories 16
    Overdiscovery 18
        Expert Testimony 18
        Novel Theory 20
        External Cause of Problems in Performance
          and Interpretation of a Contract 23
        Groundless Claims 24
    Isolated or Single Occurrence of Misuse or
        Abuse of Discovery 27

IV. DISCOVERY PROBLEMS PERCEIVED BY OPPOSING ATTORNEYS AND JUDGES 30

    Resistance to Discovery 30
    Overdiscovery 32
    Case Studies: Relationships Between Opponents'
        Perceptions and Discovery Problems 34

V.	DIFFERENCES BETWEEN THE RESISTANCE CASES AND THE OVERDISCOVERY CASES	40

      Amount of Discovery. 42
      Distribution of Discovery Between Reporting
        and Opposing Counsel. 43
      Amount of Time for Discovery and Case Disposition   44
      Motions to Compel Discovery 44
      Motions for Protective Orders 46
      Motions for Sanctions 47
      The Ad Damnum 49
      The Number of Parties 49

VI.	FACTORS AFFECTING DISCOVERY PROBLEMS	50

      The Parties and Their Relationship 50
        Relative Resources of Parties 50
        Motive for Bringing Suit or Defending an Action . . . 51
        Animosity Between the Parties 51
        Substantial Interest Beyond the Claim Itself 52
        Multiple Parties 52
      The Attorneys and the Law Firms 53
        Comparative Experience of Opposing Attorneys 53
        Comparative Degree of Specialization 54
        Protection Against Legal Malpractice Claims 54
        Comparative Attorney Styles 55
        Acrimony Between the Attorneys 56
        Acquaintance of the Opposing Attorneys 56
        Relative Size of Law Firms 57
        Comparative Law Firm Styles 58
      The Attorney's Relationship to the Client 59
        The Attorney's Control Over the Case 59
        Direct Contact Between Attorney and Client 59
        Organizational Problems in Coordinating Responses . . 60
        The Fee Arrangement 60
      The Judge and Judicial Procedures 61
        The Judge's Knowledge and Experience 61
        Extent of Judicial Control and Early Involvement . . . 61
      Case Characteristics 65
        The Timing of the Decision to Sue 65
        The Claim for Relief 66

Frivolous Claims		66
Novel Theory		66
Counterclaims		67
Expert Testimony		67
The Ad Damnum		68
Peripheral Participants		68
The Rules of Civil Procedure		69

VII. CONCLUSIONS AND RECOMMENDATIONS 72

    Conclusions 72
        Differences Between Resistance and Overdiscovery
          Cases 73
        Differences in Solutions 75
        The Nature of Discovery Abuse 76
        Professionalism and Ethics 76
        Judicial Awareness of Costs 77
        Broader Implications 77
    Recommendations 78

APPENDIX. Case Studies 82

LIST OF TABLES

1. Lawyers' Responses to Telephone Survey 6
2. Problem Cases According to Case Type and Party 7
3. Average Number of Discovery Events 42
4. Average Elapsed Time 44
5. Motions to Compel Discovery 45
6. Motions for Protective Orders 47
7. Motions for Sanctions 48

I. INTRODUCTION

The proper scope of discovery and the effect of discovery on the costs of litigation in civil cases have been controversial issues since the concept of notice pleading was introduced.[1] The modern role of discovery, effectuated in the 1938 Federal Rules of Civil Procedure, continues to draw detractors and supporters. Surprisingly, there is little difference between the arguments of the 1930s and those of the 1970s. Nevertheless, these arguments have taken on new dimensions in recent years because of

---

1. See, e.g., Proceedings of Washington and New York Institutes on the Federal Rules of Civil Procedure 39-52 (E. Hammond ed., A.B.A. 1938); Proceedings of Cleveland, Ohio Institute on the Federal Rules of Civil Procedure (A.B.A. 1938); Finch, Some Fundamental and Practical Objections to the Preliminary Draft of Rules of Civil Procedure for District Courts of the United States, 22 A.B.A.J. 809 (1936); Comment, Tactical Use and Abuse of Depositions Under the Federal Rules, 59 Yale L.J. 117 (1949).

The volume and costs of discovery are necessarily related to the scope of the claim in the complaint. There is likely to be more discovery in complex litigation and in cases where the issues have not been well defined. For discussions of the effects of pleading on the scope of discovery, see Clark, Special Pleading in the "Big Case," 23 F.R.D. 45 (1957); Clark, Comment on Judge Dawson's Paper on the Place of the Pleading in a Proper Definition of the Issues in the "Big Case," 23 F.R.D. 435 (1957); Dawson, The Place of the Pleading in a Proper Definition of the Issues in the "Big Case," 23 F.R.D. 430 (1957); Fee, The Lost Horizon in Pleading Under the Federal Rules of Civil Procedure, 49 Colum. L. Rev. 491 (1948); Simpson, The Pleading Problem, 53 Harv. L. Rev. 169, 192-206 (1939).

In the 1970s, renewed controversy has arisen over the need to control the undue expense and burden of discovery. See, e.g., Kirkham, Complex Litigation--Have Good Intentions Gone Awry?, 70 F.R.D. 199, 202-04 (1976); Liman, The Quantum of Discovery vs. the Quality of Justice: More is Less, 4 Litigation 8 (Fall 1977); Umin, Discovery Reform: A New Era or Business as Usual, 65 A.B.A.J. 1050 (1979).

the increasing costs of litigation and the fact that discovery accounts for a substantial portion of the costs of civil litigation.

These concerns prompted our study. Although preliminary planning for research projects on discovery had started in 1975, the strongest impetus for Federal Judicial Center research was the so-called Pound Revisited Conference of 1976,[2] at which discovery was highlighted as a particularly serious cost problem.

By the summer of 1978, published Center research concerning discovery included a statistically based study of cases in six districts[3] and a study that surveyed and analyzed all critical literature on the federal discovery rules published since January 1970 (the year of the last major revision of the federal discovery rules).[4] The instant project is one of the Center's continuing studies of the operation of discovery.

The Center's first discovery report was--as noted above--a statistical study. Although statistics provide information that illuminates or defines problems, some questions are more usefully addressed through case studies. The present study involves such questions.

Our interest was in obtaining more information on the nature and extent of discovery abuse. Asking directly about such abuse, however, would require attorneys to accuse opponents of misconduct.[5] Asking only for cases in which discovery was a problem, on the other hand, could

---

2. The major addresses are in National Conference on the Causes of Popular Dissatisfaction with the Administration of Justice, 70 F.R.D. 79-246 (1976).

3. P. Connolly, E. Holleman, & M. Kuhlman, Judicial Controls and the Civil Litigative Process: Discovery (Fed. Judicial Center 1978).

4. D. Segal, Survey of the Literature on Discovery from 1970 to the Present: Expressed Dissatisfactions and Proposed Reforms (Fed. Judicial Center 1978).

5. Memorandum from Joseph L. Ebersole to Federal Judicial Center Civil Litigation Committee (Mar. 31, 1978) (on file at Fed. Judicial Center).

elicit responses that were not related to problems with the federal rules--
for instance, great geographical distance. We therefore decided to
first ask attorneys to identify cases in which the burden of discovery was
disproportionate to the amount at issue. If this initial question did not
prompt an attorney to identify a case, we expanded the question. The
second part was ". . . or, have you had a case where discovery was a
problem?" The third part was ". . . or, have you had a case in which
there was abuse or attempted abuse of the discovery process?" We
planned, through this series of questions, to identify litigation that lawyers
regarded as having involved some discovery problem. Our objective was
to learn about the nature of the problem, its causes, and possible solutions.
In doing so, we hoped to understand better the role of the federal rules
in discovery. When do they contribute to the problem and when to the
solution? What changes might hold promise?

II. THE SURVEY

Methodology

Because our primary interest was in discovery problems that arise under the federal rules of civil procedure, the survey was directed to attorneys who litigate civil cases in federal courts. Recognizing that state court cases might also be called to our attention because most attorneys practice in both forums, we decided to examine state cases if the state's civil rules were modeled after the federal rules.

The clerk of the United States district court that was selected for the survey circulated the local bar association's membership list to the courtroom deputies for the district judges. The deputies were asked to underline the names of attorneys who frequently argued civil cases and seemed knowledgeable and well prepared when they appeared in court.

A single membership list was circulated among all the deputy clerks in turn so that each deputy clerk saw the selections other deputies had made previously. Although we realized that the clerks would have some biases, we thought that the number of clerks making the selections would offset the biases.

The clerks' selections produced a list of 429 attorneys. Using a pattern of random selection, we called each lawyer on the list and asked the lawyer to identify litigation in which the costs or burdens of discovery seemed disproportionately large considering the legal issue involved, or in which problems with discovery occurred, or in which there seemed to have been abuse or attempted abuse of the discovery process. We used each of these questions in turn until the respondent replied, but did not keep a record of the question that prompted the reply. The general nature of the inquiry allowed the respondents considerable latitude in selecting cases, but since the identification of problems depends to a great extent on perceptions, this latitude seemed both desirable and necessary.

As explained in later portions of this chapter, we eventually narrowed the number of cases that reportedly involved discovery problems to a selection of cases for study. We personally interviewed the attorneys who reported that selection of cases and, whenever possible, we also interviewed opposing counsel and judges.

Survey Results

Early in the survey, responses indicated the attorneys' ways of thinking about discovery problems. They tended to think first about the subject areas of their practice. Even when the lawyers had no case to report, they mentioned antitrust, construction contracts, employment discrimination, and medical malpractice as being likely to produce problems. More than 80 percent of the problem cases were reported by attorneys who participated in them, although the questions encouraged respondents to identify any cases they knew about that had involved discovery problems.

Out of the 429 attorneys telephoned, we were able to make contact with 246 who handled civil cases. Of these, 51, or approximately 21 percent, did not know of any problem cases. The results of this survey are shown in table 1.

Only four respondents claimed to be able to identify instances of actual "abuse" of the discovery rules. As shown in table 1, 50 percent of the respondents with whom we made contact identified problem cases, and most of them initially classified the problems according to the substantive areas of the law involved.

Table 2 shows the distribution of these initial classifications according to attorneys for the defendant or for the plaintiff. Of these 108 cases, 42 percent were reported by defendants' attorneys and 43 percent by plaintiffs' attorneys--an evenly divided distribution. The remaining 16 percent (figures do not add because of rounding) were cases in which the respondent reportedly represented a witness or an intervening party, or did not participate in the case.

TABLE 1

LAWYERS' RESPONSES TO TELEPHONE SURVEY
(429 Telephone Calls)

	Number	Percentage[a]
No contact	142	--
Contact	287	--
Not civil litigators	41	--
Civil litigators	246	
Had not had problem cases	51	21
Had heard of problem cases, referred to other attorney	27	11
Would "think about it" and call back	46	19
Reported problem cases	122	50
Antitrust	19	8
Personal injury	16	7
Medical malpractice	12	5
Title VII	10	4
Construction	10	4
Contract disputes[b]	8	3
Airline bumping cases	5	2
Securities	4	2
Political campaign litigation	3	--
Trademark/patents	3	--
Labor law	3	--
Engineer/architectural liability	2	--
Banking law	2	--
Bankruptcy	2	--
Alien property litigation	1	--
Attorney malpractice	1	--
Energy law	1	--
Federal tort claims	1	--
Government contracts	1	--
Landlord-tenant	1	--
Limited partnerships	1	--
Prisoners' rights	1	--
Railroad valuation	1	--
No specific case	14	6

[a]Percentage of 246 respondents computed in this column. Rounding results to a total of 101%. Percentages of 1% or less are denoted by (--).

[b]These cases include one described as an insurance contract case.

TABLE 2

PROBLEM CASES ACCORDING TO CASE TYPE AND PARTY

	Plaintiff	Defendant	Other[a]
Antitrust	5	12	2
Personal injury	10	5	1
Medical malpractice	7	4	1
Title VII	7	2	1
Construction	3	6	1
Contract disputes	5	2	1
Airline bumping cases	1	3	1
Securities	2	1	1
Political campaign litigation	1	2	--
Trademark/patents	2	1	--
Labor law	--	3	--
Engineer/architectural liability	--	2	--
Banking law	--	2	--
Bankruptcy	--	--	2
Other	3	--	6
TOTAL	46	45	17

[a] Attorneys reporting cases in this column represented a witness or an intervening party, or did not participate in the case.

The distribution of these responses according to case type should be interpreted with caution, because the same responses might have been given if the opponent in a given case had been the first attorney to be called. In that event, the percentages of plaintiff versus defendant responses would have been different, thus leading to a different inference. As a matter of fact, table 1 and the third column in table 2 show that some cases were first identified by third parties who were not part of the case but had heard about it.

Tables 1 and 2 do not represent our conclusions, but they do show the wide range of case types reported and the even balance between plaintiffs' and defendants' attorneys responding. Of the 122 attorneys who reported problem cases, 99 were either (1) inaccessible during the interview period,[6] (2) reporting cases in a state court not using the federal rules, or (3) reporting cases that turned out to be pending final disposition.[7] We scheduled follow-up interviews with attorneys reporting 23 cases; those cases were selected for study. Although all of our respondents' names were obtained from one federal district, the cases selected for study were from seven federal districts and one state court.

The attorneys who reported the 23 cases had been personally involved in each case. The distribution of subject matter was: medical malpractice (5), construction contracts (3), private antitrust (2), commercial contracts (3), personal injury or products liability (2), political campaign and election cases (1), professional liability (2), airline bumping policy (2),

---

6. As used here, inaccessibility includes refusal to be interviewed, inability to obtain a client's permission to speak with us, and geographical remoteness.

7. The Federal Judicial Center has long had a policy of not conducting research on cases still before a court. In the present study, excluding pending cases meant excluding cases that had not yet been to trial or in which an opinion had not been rendered. Cases on appeal in which pretrial issues were not appealed and the briefs were filed, however, were not absolutely excluded; they were instead considered for inclusion on a case-by-case basis.

banking law (1), and employment discrimination (2). This distribution was similar to that of the initial 122 cases reported as having discovery problems. The facts of each of the 23 cases are described in chapters three and four; the Appendix gives more detail about 6 of the cases.

III. DISCOVERY PROBLEMS PERCEIVED BY REPORTING ATTORNEYS

Most of the attorneys who identified cases in response to the questions asked in the telephone survey did so only after all three parts of the question had been posed. Thus it was not always clear which of the three parts an attorney was answering. In most instances, attorneys seemed to respond to the total question, identifying cases in which discovery had not proceeded as they felt it should have. When it was clear that an attorney thought the amount of discovery was disproportionate, that assertion was phrased generally; the attorneys responding to this part of the question did not offer any estimate of an appropriate relationship between the prayer and the cost of discovery. Discovery was described as disproportionate in terms of being more than was necessary or involving greater costs than necessary.

After the initial set of interviews, we divided the cases into those in which the problem turned on one specific discovery issue; those with pervasive discovery problems, but not a large volume of discovery; and those with pervasive discovery problems and a large volume of discovery. Several cases did not fit neatly into any of these categories, and we placed them in a sui generis category. As we reviewed the types of discovery problems reported by attorneys, however, we began to look at other possible categorizations that might be more useful for evaluation purposes. We divided cases into those that involved perceived resistance to discovery, those that involved perceived overdiscovery, and those that involved a single or isolated instance of perceived misuse of a discovery device. This grouping of cases worked well for discussion; it also had some interesting statistical features, as discussed in chapter five.

Resistance to Discovery

We subdivided resistance cases into four categories: general resistance, assertion of a privilege, resistance to document production, and resistance to interrogatories. These groups are neither rigid nor mutually exclusive; however, they generally reflect the primary problem of resistance perceived by the attorney reporting the case. The descriptions of cases in the remainder of this chapter reflect the perceptions of the reporting attorneys.

General Resistance

In two cases, general resistance occurred throughout the discovery period. One was an employment discrimination case in which a female plaintiff had been passed over for promotion to a supervisory position, but was asked to train the male who had been chosen for the position. The defense resisted every discovery initiative by the plaintiff. The plaintiff's attorney said that "the opposing attorney was very difficult to deal with." Two motions to compel discovery (rule 37(a)) were filed; both were granted. In response, the defendant employer provided plaintiff's counsel with all the personnel records. The records were in a large room that contained all the employer's files, and the defendant refused to organize them. With pro bono assistance from some recent law school graduates, the plaintiff's attorney, who was with a public interest law firm, screened all the employment records, including records of interviews with applicants who had been rejected. Many of the files contained written sexist comments by the personnel director. With this evidence, the plaintiff moved quickly to settlement.

In the second case, the administrator of a deceased woman's estate was suing a public mental hospital, claiming that the hospital's negligence in releasing the decedent's husband was the proximate cause of her murder by the husband shortly after his release. When the plaintiff tried to discover hospital records, the government claimed the doctor-patient privilege. The plaintiff's attorney then obtained a release from the husband, who was back in the mental hospital. The government then claimed a conflict of interest because of a phrase in the release. Thereafter, the government resisted discovery on a work product claim and demanded that the plaintiff children (there were nine minor children at the time of the woman's death) pay an expert witness fee for a deposition of the publicly employed doctor. The plaintiff's attorney gave these actions, which occurred several times in the case and resulted in extensive delays, as examples of the difficulties in discovery. The plaintiff finally won, but the attorney noted that the nine children grew up during the pretrial period. "By the time we got the money, it was too late to help the kids. The boys were criminals--they weren't children anymore."

Assertion of a Privilege

In one case, the reporting attorney perceived the assertion of a privilege by the opposing party as purely dilatory and obstructive. The case was a malicious prosecution suit in which the plaintiff was trying to determine whether the defendant would claim advice of counsel as a defense. The defendant refused to answer any questions on the matter, invoking the attorney-client privilege. The plaintiff needed to know whether this defense would be raised at trial because if it were, the trial would have to be recessed and the defendant further deposed at that time. The problem was solved when the judge granted a motion to compel election between either (1) raising the defense and waiving the privilege, or (2) invoking t privilege with the consequence that the defense could not be raised. The plaintiff's attorney cited this instance as an example of a serious discovery problem that would have had a purely dilatory effect had it not been solved through the motion and resulting court order.[8]

---

8. When a party has deliberately included the advice of counsel as an issue in the action, the courts have consistently held that the attorney-client privilege is waived regarding communications and documents relating

Resisting Document Production

Four cases were reported as involving resistance to document production. In the first case, the plaintiff was the wife of a man who had been killed in an automobile accident while driving a rented car. The accident occurred in an area where the highway was under construction. The defendants in this wrongful death action were the car rental company and its parent corporation, the driver of the other vehicle and his employer (the driver was on a business trip), the highway construction company, and the state highway department.

The car rental company and its parent were represented by counsel retained by the insurer. (The local franchise holder of the car rental company, from whom the decedent had rented the car, was bankrupt and therefore was not sued.) Because the shoulder restraining harness was missing from the car at the time of the accident, the plaintiff filed a request for production of documents relating to the testing and maintenance records for the car; any customer complaints about it; and the rental company's maintenance and operation manuals, hiring and training manuals, and business policy papers. The plaintiff sought the manuals and policy papers in order to find out if the rental agency had, for example, instructed employees not to check seat belts or to cut them out if they were not functioning properly. The maintenance records for the car were the only documents produced.

The plaintiff made several attempts to help obtain the other documents. The defendant's attorney said that the insurance company adjustors had searched for the documents (unsuccessfully) at the franchisee's warehouse. The plaintiff agreed to meet the defendant's agents at another warehouse, but found it deserted. Shortly thereafter, a motion to compel

---

to such advice. Haymes v. Smith, 73 F.R.D. 572, 577 (W.D.N.Y. 1976); Handgards, Inc. v. Johnson & Johnson, 413 F. Supp. 926, 929 (N.D. Cal. 1976); Garfinkle v. Arcata National Corp., 64 F.R.D. 688, 689 (S.D.N.Y. 1974); Smith v. Bentley, 9 F.R.D. 489, 490 (S.D.N.Y. 1949).

production resulted in an order to produce the manuals in three weeks. (This was during the eighth month of litigation, and the initial request for production had been filed at the time the complaint was filed.) The documents were still not produced.

Later, in inquiring about the relationship between the corporate parent, the car rental subsidiary, and its franchisees, the plaintiff learned that records of the local franchisee had been tied up in another suit, and that they had been destroyed some time during the pendency of the instant case. The plaintiff thereupon filed a motion for sanctions urging a default judgment against the corporate parent and car rental subsidiary. The court denied the request for a default judgment, but did award the plaintiff $55,000 in attorney's fees.

Another case was somewhat unusual because the discovery itself was part of the remedy the plaintiff sought. A public interest group sued an election campaign committee, claiming failure to disclose contributions as required by statute. The plaintiff requested lists of contributors. The suit was filed shortly before an election, so speedy discovery was essential to the plaintiff. Resistance involved requests for protective orders and other legal maneuvering that, in the opinion of the plaintiff's attorney, had a purely dilatory objective and were a misuse of the protective provisions of the civil rules.

A third case involved problems in obtaining a copy of an insurance policy. The plaintiff was an artist whose works were loaned for exhibit at a museum (the defendant). When the paintings were returned after the exhibit, the plaintiff discovered damage to five paintings. The two major issues were (1) the extent of damage to the five paintings and (2) whether the museum's insurance policy was a "valued" policy. If it were a valued policy, the amount to be paid in case of total destruction would be the amount shown on the policy, rather than the appraised value.

The plaintiff's discovery included the use of experts to determine the extent of damage (that is, whether the paintings were a total loss or could be restored) and interrogatories and requests for production to determine the type of insurance policy. The insurer for the museum retained counsel located in the same city as the plaintiff, and this counsel worked through a claims adjustor in the city where the museum was located. In response to interrogatories, the insurance company asserted that the policy in question was not a valued policy and that the value of the paintings had to be determined through traditional appraisal methods. The defendant's attorney reported problems in finding the insurance contract and the endorsement covering the exhibit of the plaintiff's paintings. The defendant had produced a sample of the contract early in the case and had suggested to the plaintiff that it would be sufficient.

After about nine months had passed, and a court order granted the plaintiff's motion to compel production, the original insurance contract and endorsement were delivered to the plaintiff. At trial, the policy was determined, as a matter of law, to be a valued policy. The jury found that the five paintings were a total loss. Judgment was rendered for the plaintiff, who was awarded the value of the paintings. The value was to be established by agreement between the artist and the museum, and recorded in the policy endorsement that had been the object of the request for production.

The fourth case in which document production reportedly was resisted was a so-called airline bumping case in which the plaintiff, who held a first-class ticket, had been denied a seat on a flight for which he had a confirmed reservation. The plaintiff alleged it was the airline's policy to overbook and not to disclose that it did so. The plaintiff also charged that the airline had upgraded several economy-class passengers to first class, which was a further cause of his being bumped, and that this reflected a policy of providing special favors to VIPs.

The plaintiff's primary thrust in discovery was to seek information about the airline's policies. This search began with interrogatories, and was later pressed through requests for production of documents and through notices of depositions accompanied by requests for production of documents at the taking of the deposition. The plaintiff's attorney believed that some of the defendant's officers intentionally failed to bring relevant documents to depositions. Further, the request for production of documents did not produce the documents that the plaintiff was requesting. In some instances, responses to requests for production of documents were that the documents were unknown or did not exist. The plaintiff's counsel reported difficulty in locating the proper airline officials to depose.

Discovery came to a standstill for twenty-two months while a case on the same legal issues wound its way from a court of appeals to the Supreme Court. After the Supreme Court decision clarified the case law, fifteen additional months of discovery ensued before a settlement was reached.

Resisting Answers to Interrogatories

Two cases involved problems with replies to interrogatories. In each case the reporting attorney perceived the problem as one of intentional evasion by the opposing side. The first case arose out of injuries that the plaintiff sustained when a rented chair he was sitting in collapsed at a catered party. Defendants included the party giver, the caterer, the chair rental company, and the chair manufacturer. The plaintiff's interrogatories included asking the manufacturer if it had ever issued any warnings that injury could result from use of the chair model in question. An officer of the manufacturer replied that the firm had not published or distributed such materials. The chair rental company and the caterer also responded that they knew of no recalls or warnings distributed by the manufacturer. Using all discovery devices, the plaintiff attempted to determine the cause of the defect, but without success.

Discovery took place over a three-year period. At the second day of trial, testimony revealed that an earlier version of the chair model in question had been recalled, and that the manufacturer had distributed warnings and recall notices. Further, testimony by the caterer indicated the possibility--contradicting responses to discovery requests--that one of the recalled chairs might have been used at the party where the plaintiff was injured. Upon receiving this testimony, the court declared a mistrial. The plaintiff's attorney then undertook further discovery and reached a settlement favorable to his client.

Resistance to interrogatories also occurred in another airline bumping case. The plaintiff sued on a count of common law misrepresentation and on a statutory claim. In discovery, he sought to determine whether the defendant airline had a corporate policy of intentionally overbooking flights. The plaintiff felt that the airline resisted discovery by giving evasive answers to interrogatories on this subject. The airline responded to three key questions as irrelevant.

After a motion to compel was granted, the airline provided revised answers. The plaintiff had asked, for example, whether the reservation or ticketing system was designed, programmed, or operated to permit acceptance of more reservations than the number of seats that were in fact available on any particular flight or flights under any circumstances. The revised response to this question was "Yes, under certain circumstances (this is done)." The same revised answer was given to the following questions: (1) Was the reservation or ticketing system designed, programmed, or operated to permit the issuance of more tickets for confirmed reserved space than the number of seats in fact available on any particular flight or flights under any circumstances? and (2) Did the airline, as a matter of corporate policy or practice, purposefully overbook certain flights on the statistical assumption that a certain percentage of ticketed passengers would not show up for any such flight? The defendant resisted the plaintiff's further efforts to obtain an answer to the last question, claiming that it was not relevant to the elements of the plaintiff's cause of action.

After a Supreme Court decision settled the law in this area, the plaintiff moved for a motion to compel answers to the interrogatories in question. The questions were answered, and the case was settled shortly thereafter.

Overdiscovery

In all the overdiscovery cases, the reporting attorney described the amount of discovery as disproportionate. We divided the eleven overdiscovery cases into those in which (1) expert testimony was all-important, (2) a novel theory or novel action was involved, (3) an external factor created problems in performance or interpretation of a contract, and (4) the defendant's attorney felt the cause was groundless.

Expert Testimony

Discovery problems were related to expert testimony in one products liability case and three medical malpractice cases. In the products liability case, the plaintiffs were mechanics at a garage. One had been the driver and the other a rider in a car being test-driven after repairs. While they were approaching a curve, the car unexpectedly accelerated. The driver lost control and the car hit a tree; both men were injured.

The plaintiffs' attorney proceeded on a general defect theory. He alleged that there was a defect in the accelerator linkage or carburetor that caused the car to accelerate uncontrollably, but he was unable to make any allegation regarding the specific defect that might have been a proximate cause of the accident.

The defense attorney, representing the automobile manufacturer, thought that the court should not have allowed discovery to continue because the plaintiffs, throughout most of the pretrial period, were unable to find an expert who could identify a specific defect that could have caused the accident. This issue pervaded the whole discovery process and led to contentiousness. The defense attorney, who believed that discovery must be confined to the issues, saw the plaintiffs' failure to identify a specific defect as an inability to define the issues, and he felt that the plaintiffs engaged in overdiscovery.

In his first interrogatories, the defense lawyer asked the plaintiffs to identify the specific defect. These were not answered until eighteen months later, after a conference with the judge. After a protracted period of discovery, only two weeks before trial, the plaintiffs' attorney located an expert who knew of a design defect that could have caused the sudden acceleration. At trial, this person was the only expert testifying for the plaintiffs. The jury returned a verdict for the plaintiffs.

In one medical malpractice case, the plaintiff had suffered a fractured leg and a punctured lung in an automobile accident. At the hospital, the doctors encountered difficulties when they tried to set his leg. During the fourth attempt, the plaintiff had a cardiac arrest. He was resuscitated and was then hospitalized for six months. The plaintiff filed a $3.75 million malpractice suit against two orthopedic surgeons, three anesthesiologists, a pulmonary specialist, a heart specialist, and the hospital.

The attorney reporting the case, who had represented one of the orthopedic surgeons, felt the case was overdiscovered. As a result of insurance coverage and the separability of charges, every one of the seven defendant doctors had an expert witness to testify for him. This led to more than fifteen depositions--none covering less than two days--and about 8,000 pages of transcript. The reporting attorney felt this was more than the case warranted, but he did not think the depositions were an abuse of discovery. Rather, he felt that interrogatories had been misused: the plaintiff's attorney had posed form interrogatories "five to seven inches thick."

Another malpractice case involved a plaintiff with a complicated history of muscular disorders; various steps had been taken to cure him. He filed a malpractice suit against two surgeons after an operation resulted in internal scarring. The operation was of a type that, according to the attorney reporting the case, could have been performed by any of three types of specialists, although each would have used slightly different techniques. The defendants' attorney believed discovery was excessive and too costly; specialists were hired and deposed to establish the standard of care and accepted practice. The defendants deposed the first four experts the plaintiff hired; the experts agreed that the defendants had done everything correctly. Three-and-a-half years after the case was filed, and only two weeks before trial, the plaintiff located an expert in one of the specialties who disagreed with the procedures that had been used. The plaintiff used this expert at trial, but the defendants received a directed verdict.

The pattern of the third malpractice case was somewhat similar to that of the second. A man who had experienced symptoms indicating internal hemorrhaging underwent emergency surgery. Although all his vital signs were excellent after surgery, he went into shock four hours later and was rushed back to surgery. On the way, he suffered cardiac arrest and was given immediate cardiopulmonary resuscitation. When the surgeons reopened his abdomen, they repaired the damaged vein they found and sewed the patient up again, but it soon became apparent that he was still bleeding internally. When they opened the abdomen for the third time, the surgeons saw that the additional internal bleeding was apparently caused by a rib that had been broken when cardiopulmonary resuscitation was administered. The doctors mended the damage but within days, infection started. Other complications developed, and the patient died two-and-a-half months later.

The man's widow sued four doctors and the hospital. Discovery included what one of the defendants' attorneys referred to as "massive" interrogatories. More than fifteen depositions were taken. The defendants deposed the plaintiff's two experts. Three weeks before trial and six months after the discovery cutoff date, the plaintiff located a third expert. The court approved this witness, but denied both sides any additional witnesses. At trial, judgment was rendered in favor of the defendants.

Novel Theory

Three overdiscovery cases involved novel legal theories. In one, a medical malpractice case, the plaintiff had been diagnosed as a schizophrenic and hospitalized in a private psychiatric hospital for five years. Later, other doctors told him his condition was organic and that it had become chronic because it had not been treated. The plaintiff claimed that the admitting and treating psychiatrists in the private hospital should have recognized the organic condition and that the treatment should have consisted of a special diet.

The suit was filed against the hospital and six psychiatrists, whose credibility the plaintiff's counsel tested at depositions by questioning them about their familiarity with strictly medical matters. The defense team included counsel for two uninsured defendants, counsel retained by three insurance carriers, and counsel retained by the hospital. (Because of the possibility that the verdict would exceed the limits of its insurance policy, the hospital had wanted separate counsel.)

One of the defendant doctors' attorneys characterized discovery in the case as primarily "Who are your experts and what are their contentions?" He reported that there was "a tremendous amount of discovery, very expensive. . . . My client couldn't afford to send me on deposition trips throughout the U. S. or to buy copies of all the transcripts."

Discovery involved establishing a national standard of care for the plaintiff's condition and searching for medical experts who would support the diagnosis of an organic condition and the untraditional approach to treatment. The process took two years. There were six sets of interrogatories and, during the six-week period before the trial, seventeen depositions of non-party experts in widely separated locations where the plaintiff had received treatment in the past. Fourteen of the depositions were noticed by the defendants, because of the plaintiff's novel medical theory and the need to establish a national standard of care. The plaintiff conducted most of his discovery well before trial, but deposed none of the defense's experts so as not to reveal his case. The trial lasted one month and resulted in a verdict for the defendants.

In the second case involving a novel theory, the plaintiff, a proprietary college, sued a nonprofit regional college accreditation association to enjoin the association's enforcement of a rule denying accreditation to any but nonprofit organizations. The plaintiff claimed that (1) the defendant and its members had formed a combination or conspiracy in restraint of the plaintiff's trade in violation of the Sherman Antitrust Act; (2) the accrediting function is so inherently governmental that it is a state action in a constitutional sense, subject to the restraint of due process; and (3) the defendant had acted in an arbitrary, discriminatory, and unreasonable manner in rejecting the college's application for accreditation.

The defendant's attorney felt the complaint was too broad and general and that the plaintiff's discovery was excessive. The three-year course of discovery seemed to him protracted and overly ideological. In his opinion, only 25 percent of the plaintiff's discovery was useful at trial.

The plaintiff's discovery addressed several issues. One set of depositions, conducted with admissions officers of schools to which the plaintiff college's students applied or transferred, was designed to show the effect of the college's unaccredited status on students' applications or transfers. Another part of discovery sought information relevant to the plaintiff's claim that higher education is part of trade or commerce. A series of depositions with government officials and others explored the effect of accreditation on federal student loans and financial aid. The plaintiff took seventeen depositions; the defendant, fifteen. The plaintiff prevailed after a two-and-a-half-month trial.

The third case that presented a novel theory arose out of a Securities and Exchange Commission (SEC) investigation that resulted in multidistrict securities fraud litigation. The SEC contended that corporations' attorneys and accountants had a duty to go to the SEC with information of securities law violations obtained in the course of representing a corporation. According to one defense attorney, discovery was conducted on a consolidated basis by a liaison committee that did not veto any discovery requested, but did act as a scheduler of possibly repetitious depositions. More than 150 depositions were taken, and more than 50,000 pages of transcript were produced. The five-year course of discovery preceded a month-long trial, but the case was hard-fought, in part because of professional liability claims that the SEC raised.

External Cause of Problems in Performance and Interpretation of a Contract

In two of the overdiscovery cases, an external factor had created problems in interpretation and performance of a contract, leading to suit. In each case--one was a supply contract and the other, a construction contract--the plaintiff's attorney reported disproportionate discovery.

The external cause in the supply contract case was the OPEC embargo and price increase. The plaintiff was a natural gas utility that sued an oil refiner for anticipatory breach of contract. The refiner was to have delivered to the utility a by-product of the oil refining process; the utility had planned to build a facility to convert the by-product to synthetic natural gas. Differences over interpretation of the contract's price terms led to the suit.

The plaintiff's attorney felt the amount of discovery by the defendant was excessive. The defendant pursued several theories--including supervening events and commercial frustration of the contract--in addition to its own interpretation of the price terms. The oil embargo had occurred after the contract was signed; the refinery used imported crude oil, but the contract's price terms were tied to the price of domestic crude oil.

Discovery by the defendant included depositions of more than 100 persons in a two-year period. Those deposed included top executives of the utility, finance houses to determine the utility's financial condition, officials of another utility that was building a similar plant, companies having knowledge of the requirements for construction of the conversion plant, and others. Two-and-a-half years after the action began, the defendant settled for $2.7 million.

The external cause in the construction contract case was a government agency's delay in approving a large number of minor orders for change in a project to renovate a group of residential apartment buildings. Construction related to the changes could not take place until the orders were approved by the government; otherwise, the contractor would be held to have waived payment for any unapproved change. Until all the changes were made, the owner, a one-transaction nonprofit corporation, couldn't pay the contractor. Thus the construction company had to continue paying interest on financing and bonds for longer than it had anticipated. Hearing that the owner planned to sue alleging incomplete and abandoned work, the construction firm decided to sue for breach of contract immediately. The firm's complaint charged, <u>inter alia</u>, that the owner had failed to provide adequate plans and had refused to offer equitable adjustment of the contract price and work schedule to compensate for its poor performance. The firm apparently filed suit one day before the owner had planned to do so. The defendant responded with a counterclaim. Under then-current law, the government agency could not be joined as a defendant.

The plaintiff was represented throughout by the same counsel in a firm of four to six lawyers. The defendant, a public corporation whose funding was derived from grants-in-aid to renovate housing for publicly subsidized occupants, was represented by a large law firm's public interest litigation team. The plaintiff's counsel felt that the defense firm "was training lawyers on this case"; discovery was sporadic, and different attorneys appeared periodically at depositions and gave answers to interrogatories. The plaintiff's counsel felt that there were many unnecessary interrogatories, depositions, and requests for production of documents. He stated that the various discovery devices covered the same material, resulting in extensive duplication. In his opinion, the defense team's inexperience with this type of dispute prolonged discovery over a two-year period and required amendments to the answer, leading in turn to further depositions as trial approached. The case was terminated by summary judgment--in favor of the defendant on the original claim and in favor of the plaintiff on the counterclaim.

<u>Groundless Claims</u>

In two overdiscovery cases, defendants' attorneys perceived the claims as groundless. One was an antitrust case, the second a construction contract case.

In the antitrust case, one of the defense attorneys believed the suit was "a real fishing expedition." Although he considered filing a malicious prosecution suit after the action was terminated, he decided against it because "in an antitrust action there is almost always something that justifies the court in allowing the action to proceed." The plaintiff, a newspaper publisher that had gone out of business, filed a $9 million private antitrust suit against several individuals and the parent organization of several newspapers that had been direct competitors of the plaintiff's newspapers. The plaintiff alleged that he was driven out of business by illegal actions of the defendants that violated the Sherman and Clayton Acts. The plaintiff's previous suit against one of the individual defendants (who had sold his newspapers to the defendant parent corporation) had been dismissed when he refused to respond to discovery requests. Because of this history, the parent corporation defendant's attorney moved for and was granted an order conditioning their obligation to respond to discovery on the plaintiff's response to discovery requests.

The defense attorney recalled that there was little discovery for the first seventeen months. Then the judge set a discovery cutoff date eight months thereafter (along with a pretrial conference date and a trial date), and discovery started in earnest. The plaintiff took lengthy depositions of thirty-one persons, resulting in more than 7,500 pages of transcript. The general manager of the defendant parent corporation, for example, was deposed for thirteen days, the head of operations for ten days. The defendant's attorney felt these depositions could have been taken in less than one-third of the time. The plaintiff's discovery also included seven sets of interrogatories, eight requests for production of documents, and long lists of requests for admissions. One day before the discovery cutoff date, the plaintiff filed a sixth and seventh set of interrogatories. The sixth set alone had more than 15,000 subparts and 120 major questions. On the same day, the plaintiff also asked the defendants to state whether any part of any prior deposition was inaccurate and if so, to state the accurate response. The defendants' attorneys considered this an abuse of the discovery process. They obtained a protective order against responding to this request and to the sixth and seventh set of interrogatories, on the grounds that they were repetitious and violated the cutoff date.

The defense conducted most of its discovery informally through investigators or paralegals. Discovery included a survey of advertisers in the relevant market areas. The longest deposition took one-and-a-half days. When the plaintiff failed to respond to document requests and to an order granting a motion to compel production, the defense deposed two accountants and three bank officials, each for half an hour.

The judge issued a lengthy pretrial order which, in the opinion of the defendant's attorney, was ideal for this type of case in that it helped the plaintiff realize he didn't have a case. The case was dismissed with prejudice shortly after the pretrial conference.

In the construction contract case, the plaintiff--a subcontractor for plumbing, heating, air-conditioning, and ventilation in a commercial office building--had sued the prime contractor for (1) interference with its work by failing to obtain the owner's approval of plans in a timely fashion, (2) delay caused by the subcontractor's having to prepare drawings and blueprints--work that was not required under the contract—and (3) the costs of defending against the subcontractor's material suppliers. The defendant's attorney stated that half the delay had been caused by the plaintiff's blueprints, which could not be used because they routed pipes and sleeves through major steel structures. This error had occurred in blueprints for each floor, and the plaintiff had to prepare new drawings each time. Because of a liquidated damages provision, the owner had withheld half the progress payments to the prime contractor, who in turn had withheld half the progress payments to the subcontractor.

The defendant's attorney felt discovery in this case was excessive and largely unnecessary because the plaintiff asked primarily for invoices and progress reports that it had sent to the defendant; a record of payments that the defendant had made to the plaintiff; and all documents related to the plaintiff's work, all because the plaintiff had no bookkeeping system. More important, the attorney believed the suit had been brought as a last resort to keep the plaintiff from going out of business, and the discovery justified the suit to the plaintiff's accountants, who were trying to assess the plaintiff's financial situation.

The defendant's attorney implied that this was a frivolous suit and that conducting discovery was a way to harrass the defendant into a payoff. The case was settled for $65,000. (The plaintiff had sued for $60,000 on its contractual claim, $225,000 on its interference and delay claims, and $25,000 on suppliers' claims.)

Isolated or Single Occurrence of Misuse or Abuse of Discovery

Three cases did not fit neatly into either the resistance or overdiscovery category. Two of the cases involved requests for production of documents that the reporting attorneys thought were improper. One of those instances was part of a much larger case, but the attorney reporting the case identified the request as the only noteworthy discovery problem in the case. In the second case with a request-for-production problem, potential overdiscovery did not occur because the plaintiff did not pursue the litigation. In the third case that was difficult to classify as either overdiscovery or resistance, a third person, not a party to the lawsuit, was involved in discovery.

The first illustration of the single-occurrence problem is a case that was initiated by an American agribusiness corporation against a large bank. The plaintiff had a contract with another country as part of an Agency for International Development (AID) project. The bank refused to pay on a letter of credit for work that the plaintiff claimed had been completed before the contract was terminated. The United States government intervened as a third-party defendant and asserted a counterclaim against the plaintiff for all moneys paid, and to be paid, plus a penalty, alleging that the plaintiff was guilty of overinvoicing.

The reported problem was that a government request for production of documents was too broad: instead of asking for all documents relating to the invoices, the government asked for every document related to the contract, whether or not it involved AID financing. The documents were in a warehouse in another state and had recently been made available to AID as part of a thorough audit AID had conducted. The plaintiff objected to the request, arguing that it was overly broad and that business secrets would be exposed in the process. The objection was refused, and two of the plaintiff's employees spent two months preparing the response. The plaintiff's attorney perceived this as an abuse of the discovery process that the judge should have prevented.

In another case, the plaintiff, a distributor of plumbing supplies, had sued the surety on a bond for goods delivered to a subcontractor for a federal government building. The subcontractor had gone out of business still owing the plaintiff money. The defendant, the surety principal, claimed that because the material that had been ordered didn't conform to the building contract requirements, the plaintiff was not due any money. The plaintiff claimed it was not responsible for examining the building contract's requirements for each order from contractors or subcontractors, but rather, that the entity placing the order must know what to order. The discovery problem occurred when the defendant asked the plaintiff, through interrogatories, to identify all contracts for which it had supplied materials in the past six years and information on the extent to which the plaintiff examined requirements in each.

The plaintiff had fifty-two branch offices and an estimated 60,000 separate sales each year to the government or government contractors. A staff of accountants would have needed months to accumulate the information requested. The plaintiff objected, and the judge held a chambers conference shortly thereafter. The judge pointed out that the parties would easily spend more on discovery than the case was worth, and he gave the attorneys his oral suggestions for settlement. The defendant settled for the full amount of the claim. The plaintiff's attorney noted that the defense attorneys were very competent; in his opinion, the judge's suggestion enabled them to convince their "hard-nosed" client that settlement was the easier course.

The third single-occurrence problem arose in a case in which discovery was initiated against a third person. The defendant in this employment discrimination suit, a state social welfare agency, made a motion to compel the non-party deponent, a newspaperman, to divulge the names of his sources for a story about the defendant agency. The action had reverse discrimination overtones; that is, the plaintiff was protesting affirmative action appointments. The plaintiff believed that discovery of the sources for the story would be beneficial for his suit. In response to a motion to compel the newspaperman to divulge his sources, the reporter's attorney claimed newsman's privilege under applicable state law as the basis for refusal. The court denied the rule 37(a) motion to compel discovery of the confidential news source. The newspaperman's attorney reported this incident as an attempt at overdiscovery.

IV. DISCOVERY PROBLEMS PERCEIVED BY OPPOSING ATTORNEYS AND JUDGES

After talking to the attorneys who reported the twenty-three cases described in chapter three, we gained another perspective by interviewing opposing counsel and judges involved in some of those cases. That second set of interviews revealed differences in perception among participants, depending on their position in the case--differences concerning the cause or definition of a discovery problem, or even the function of discovery in general. In both resistance and overdiscovery cases, these differences in perception were accompanied by another factor: one party made an initial miscalculation of its opposition, which was compounded by some loss of client control by counsel, the inexpert use of discovery techniques, or relative inexperience with the substantive law involved in the case.

Resistance to Discovery

Interviews with opposing counsel in resistance cases showed that discovery problems were related to misunderstanding of an opposing counsel's relationship with his client, a perception that the other party was uncooperative, or an accusation of intentional resistance. In the wrongful death action involving a man who was killed while driving a rented car, the plaintiff's counsel's initial feeling was that his opponent's clients were covering up evidence regarding their maintenance and operating procedures for rental cars. He was incredulous to learn that the defense counsel saw the problem as an organizational one: coordinating the responses of the former parent corporation of the car rental agency, its insurer, and an uncooperative franchisee. The defense counsel first saw his role as a relayer of information from these various sources; then (once the incredulity of the plaintiff's counsel was apparent to him) as an organizer of that information; and finally (after the fury of the plaintiff's counsel was evident), as an independent investigator of the clients' actions.

Another resistance case involved an airline's bumping a honeymoon couple; there was only one seat left on the flight in question. The plaintiff's counsel described the case as the airline bumping case in which discovery was the most difficult, because the defendant resisted answering three interrogatories that it claimed were not relevant to facts pertaining to the flight. Two of those questions concerned the airline's computerized reservations system, and one dealt with its corporate policy on overbooking. The plaintiff's counsel thought that the questions were neutral in tone; the airline's outside counsel thought they imputed a malevolent purpose to a reservation system designed to do no more than fill an airplane with passengers. The lawyers' differing perceptions, then, involved the purpose of the reservation system. The defense counsel resisted the three interrogatories because he felt the questions were of poor quality and overly broad; how, he asked, can a computer system have an "intent" or "purpose"? This perception--that plaintiff's counsel could not or would not ask the right questions--infected the defense team's relationship with the plaintiff's counsel when the latter felt compelled to resort to depositions to get information.

A second airline bumping case was also handled by outside counsel for the defendant airline, but in this case the defense counsel attributed much of the delay to the time required for his communications with the airline's in-house legal counsel and its insurer, both of whom were supervising his conduct of the case. But the perceptions of the cause of delay in this case were at wide variance: plaintiff's counsel thought the delay was due to their difficulty in locating the proper airline official to depose, which they at first tried to do by interrogatory.

In the employment discrimination case, the plaintiff's counsel thought the defense resisted his gaining access to employment records. The plaintiff was subsequently given free access, but had to organize the records.

The plaintiff's counsel said he was always hesitant to call the defense counsel because of the latter's obdurate posture. The defendant's counsel, on the other hand, thought that the requests were too broad and so saw little value in reviewing the records. The dispute turned on the question of which party should have the burden of organizing the employment records in the first such suit against the defendant. The judge thought that the defense was "stonewalling" the plaintiff's counsel.

Overdiscovery

In the resistance cases in which we interviewed opposing counsel, differences in attorneys' styles of lawyering seemed to account for many of the problems the lawyers reported. In the overdiscovery cases, on the other hand, substantive problems of law loomed larger. Either the legal theory underlying the complaint seemed novel--at least for the jurisdiction involved--or a poorly drafted contract contained ambiguities that not only provoked litigation, but also invited discovery concerning the events or business relationships surrounding the contracts.

The products liability case that involved two mechanics who were injured in a car they were test-driving engendered a dispute over the specificity required in the pleadings. The plaintiff pleaded a general defect theory. The defense counsel thought follow-up discovery was too broad; the plaintiff's counsel considered it a legitimate mechanism for uncovering the cause of the automobile accident and finding an expert who could pinpoint the cause. The plaintiff's counsel thought this was necessary not in order to make a legally sufficient case, but to strengthen his case before the jury. From the defense counsel's perspective, however, the plaintiff should not have been allowed to proceed without either pleading or responding more specifically to the defense's interrogatories. Opposing counsel, then, disagreed over the function of and relationship between the pleadings and the discovery process. Moreover, each party thought the other was holding back, and the judge thought both were.

In another case in which overdiscovery was the initially perceived problem, the former patient suing a private psychiatric hospital for an alleged misdiagnosis rested his case on a novel theory. The bulk of discovery was by deposition conducted in widely dispersed locations and just preceding a discovery cutoff date: the plaintiff's counsel--a sole practitioner specializing in criminal defense work--perceived this as an attempt to keep him from his other cases. The defense counsel asserted that any medical malpractice defense requiring the presentation of a standard of care also requires wide-ranging discovery regarding a plaintiff's medical history and a doctor's past experience with similar diagnoses. The plaintiff and defense attorneys differed over how large a community of experts was needed in the case; the defense, who felt there was a need to establish a national standard of care, emphasized the use of national experts. Furthermore, the defense thought one of the plaintiff's witnesses was very effective and had to be countered. The plaintiff's counsel saw discovery as giving away one's case before trial, while the defense saw it as trial preparation.

Similarly, the private antitrust suit brought by a proprietary college against a nonprofit regional accreditation board was handled by attorneys with very different perceptions of the function of discovery. Because the suit was a novel one with ideological overtones, the plaintiff's counsel thought that familiarity with educational institutions and the attitudes of educators could best be gleaned from depositions; the defense counsel, on the other hand, thought hotly debated, ideological issues could best be objectively evaluated by interrogatories and document production. The defense attorney viewed most of the discovery as unnecessary, because in his opinion the theory was ideological and not based on valid legal grounds. The plaintiff's attorney felt the discovery was absolutely essential for preparing a case that, in addition to resting on a novel theory, would determine the survival of his client, the college. The judge agreed that the amount of discovery the plaintiff conducted was justified in this case.

In three contract disputes, the opposing counsel's perceptions were based on the ambiguities of the contracts. The suit by the natural gas utility against an oil refiner for anticipatory breach of a supply contract involved different opinions about the nature of the dispute. The plaintiff thought the case could be tried quickly because the basic question was whether a series of events culminated in a breach of contract. The defense, however, felt the case was amenable to more protracted discovery because additional issues, concerning the parties' ability to perform the contract, were to be tried as well.

A second contract dispute involved a construction contract in which opposing counsel, in interpreting the contract, gave differing emphasis to defective work, job delays, and work-schedule changes. The dispute was not atypical; the question was who should bear the risk of job changes and delays--the general contractor or the subcontractor--if the contract is silent on such matters. A third contract dispute, also a construction case, was similar, except that the parties' disagreement turned on the question of who should prepare new blueprints made necessary by changes in the job.

Case Studies: Relationships Between Opponents' Perceptions and Discovery Problems

Of the four resistance cases and six overdiscovery cases discussed previously in this chapter, six provide particularly clear examples of how participants' differing perceptions combine with other factors to create discovery problems. These six cases, five of which reportedly involved overdiscovery, show that the problem-causing characteristics of a case are often exacerbated by inadequate communication between counsel. The full details of these cases are given in the Appendix.

Framing the pleadings took six months in Profett College v. Area Accrediting Association. Discovery began with a "first wave" of interrogatories, but it did not become a problem for the two attorneys involved until the number of depositions became excessive. The plaintiff's counsel thought many depositions of college officials would provide data on the standards applied by other colleges to Profett transfer students and graduates. The defense, however, generally favored limiting discovery to interrogatories and document requests, as in English law practice--particularly in this type of case. Profett involved an innovative use of the federal antitrust statutes and a novel theory of due process; the discovery issues had ideological overtones involving the private sector's ability to deliver educational services and the quasi-public function of accreditation.

The plaintiff's counsel thought it was important to hear and see officials involved in the questions of higher education. Although the defense did not agree, he did think that the plaintiff's discovery was equally beneficial for his case. Both counsel remembered the deposition travel as the only time they saw each other face-to-face during the pretrial period. Both worked in relatively small law offices, and when they were involved with other cases, discovery in the Profett litigation tended to halt for weeks at a time.

Both counsel in Stuffing Pipe Association v. Prime Construction, Inc. worked in law firms that specialized in construction contract disputes. Both thought that most of the discovery could be limited to interrogatories and document requests. Although the issues raised in discovery seemed typical, the plaintiff's counsel thought that the litigation was somewhat unusual in that a financially hard-pressed subcontractor was suing a general contractor.

The problems with discovery came in two phases. Early problems turned on whether the defense should respond to document requests made necessary by the plaintiff's failure to keep records. Motions to compel answers to interrogatories and document requests were mooted by compromises worked out between counsel. Midway through discovery, the plaintiff's counsel deposed the defendant's job-site manager; this was the only deposition noticed in the case.

In the second phase, the defense moved to add a counterclaim to its complaint. This motion was accompanied by further interrogatories and document requests. The plaintiff's counsel had expected such a motion earlier, but he thought it was made too close to the trial date that had already been set. He opposed the motion, pushing for an early trial for his financially strapped clients, while the defense sought discovery to support the counterclaim. The defense thought that the plaintiff's sole remaining asset was its cause of action. When the motion to amend the complaint was granted and discovery was allowed to proceed for three more months, counsel began settlement discussions. They negotiated a settlement before the postponed trial date.

Gibbs v. Autoco, Inc. was a personal injury and products liability case arising out of a one-car automobile accident. The plaintiff's counsel thought discovery was precipitated by a legally sufficient, but too general, set of pleadings. This generality, he thought, necessitated several attempts to understand the mechanics of the malfunctioning automobile. His first experts failed to come up with an explanation for the malfunction and, after that, he took on the job himself. Most of his tests on the car were performed outside the discovery process; they only highlighted the problems with prior discovery, which had involved frustrated attempts to perform the same tests.

The defense counsel took a very different view: from the outset, he perceived discovery as a battle of experts that was not fought because the plaintiff's counsel was unable to explain, through experts or otherwise, the exact cause of the malfunction. The defense had no explanation to counter.

The judge took a third view. He perceived both counsel to be "under wraps"; that is, holding down the volume of discovery at their clients' request.

Counsel for both sides said that in some respects, such as production of photographs of the accident, they cooperated with each other. Each regarded the other as well qualified in the substantive law and litigation techniques required for handling the case. Once both counsel conceded that the trial would be a battle of experts speculating on the cause of the accident, discovery conducted just before trial proceeded smoothly.

After some initial problems in framing the complaint, the defense conducted discovery in Pease v. The Psychometric Institute to establish a national standard of care for the defendant psychiatrists treating the plaintiff. The three defense counsel felt this approach was necessitated by the applicable substantive law. In their opinion, the fact that most of the depositions occurred in a concentrated period of time was a matter of coincidence; the sole practitioner plaintiff's counsel regarded it as an attempt to keep him away from his other cases. Moreover, the plaintiff's counsel thought that in general, discovery of the other side's experts and witnesses only tended to reveal one's own case and enable the defense to organize in response.

The lead defense counsel's general approach to defense work was to first take a deposition of the plaintiff to "size him up." This strategy also revealed the other defense lawyers' different styles of questioning, ranging from informational to argumentative. One defense attorney thought that the plaintiff made a poor impression at the first deposition; thereafter, he saw discovery as a battle of experts and his role on the defense team as recruiter of the best experts. Another attorney (representing uninsured defendants) thought there was too much discovery and too little time spent discussing a negotiated settlement. The lead defense counsel saw the lengthy deposition process as a necessary follow-up to the first deposition's disclosures about the plaintiff's medical history.

All three defense attorneys denied being overbearing to the plaintiff's counsel, but the judge in the case thought the defense conducted elaborate discovery with overwhelmingly superior resources.

Smith v. Ajax, Inc. was a wrongful death action that arose after a rented car and a truck crashed at a highway construction site. The plaintiff's counsel at first viewed the action as a products liability case involving a faulty steering wheel. The counsel for one of the defendants, the automobile manufacturer, resisted this view and insisted on specific interrogatories about the car's malfunctioning. In response, the plaintiff's counsel gradually shifted the focus of his discovery to the car rental company, represented by a partner in a much smaller law office. The plaintiff's counsel thought this attorney was dilatory at best, and at worst engaged in a cover-up of the company's operating manuals. From this defense counsel's point of view, some inconsistent responses about the manuals' existence and location were the result of poor communication between himself, the franchisor car rental company, its insurer, its parent company, and its (uncooperative) former franchisee.

The communication problems on the defense side were resolved gradually when the insurance company and corporate counsel took over supervision of the defense. But by then, the results of further depositions had reinforced the plaintiff's counsel in his view that there was a cover-up. The plaintiff's counsel made two motions for default judgment on grounds that the defense had failed to respond to his discovery requests: both motions were ultimately denied, but the expenses and costs involved were assessed against the defendant. The plaintiff's counsel continued to stress the "smoking gun" aspects of the information he sought in the manuals, and he pressed discovery further. The defense thought their admittedly inconsistent results in responding nonetheless showed a continuous, good-faith effort to respond and to coordinate the efforts of a massive corporate structure. They considered their lead counsel so devastated by the discovery process, however, that for the ensuing trial, they hired a litigation partner in a law firm not previously involved in the case.

The new lead defense attorney thought most of the discovery was irrelevant to the issues that were tried. This view was bolstered by the defense attorney for the highway construction company, who was trying to use discovery to share what was initially perceived as the construction firm's liability. The firm wanted to establish shared liability among the truck driver, the truck's owner (and the driver's employer), and the construction company; the car rental company was not at all involved in the verdict and judgment for the plaintiff.

Gastex, Inc. v. Amonil, Inc. arose out of an ambiguous price term in a supply contract between a major oil producer and a public utility. The utility, which sued the producer to enforce the contract, was represented by two outside counsel from a firm specializing in general litigation--one handled the written material and the other, the oral arguments in the case. Both outside counsel felt the question to be answered by discovery was whether a breach of contract had occurred. The defense attempted to soften the plaintiff's sharp focus on this issue by raising additional questions: whether the plaintiff had the capacity to take delivery of and use the supplies called for in the contract, the impact of federal energy regulations on the contract, and the effect of the intervening 1973 OPEC oil embargo. Afraid of going to trial on a single issue before a jury in the plaintiff's service area, the defense (a somewhat larger law firm that occasionally used as many as twenty attorneys on the case) took more than a hundred depositions to bolster its position. Some associates on the defense team, however, thought that this effort was misdirected--in part because of the prior legal specialty of the supervising partner. This partner and the firm were developing a new specialty in energy law.

The plaintiff's two outside counsel considered three-quarters of the defense's discovery to be necessary, but the plaintiff's in-house counsel disagreed: he thought that the defense's effort was focused on the wrong time period and that if the same net had been cast over a wider range, the results would have been measurably more productive for the defense.

The plaintiff's outside counsel soon realized that their view of the case was too simple, but throughout discovery they thought that their principal task was to proceed, without the aid of paralegals or other support staff, to the jury trial. Some of their own documentary discovery was, they thought, helpful in establishing a course of corporate conduct leading up to the events allegedly constituting a breach of contract, but they continued to resist the expansion of discovery concerning their client's corporate planning to carry out the contract.

The fundamental difference between opposing counsel in this case was their varying emphasis on the alleged breach as opposed to the circumstances surrounding the contract's implementation. The effects of this difference were heightened by the great differences between the law firms' organization.

V. DIFFERENCES BETWEEN THE RESISTANCE CASES AND THE OVERDISCOVERY CASES

The comments of the participants we interviewed indicated substantive differences between cases that had resistance problems and those that involved overdiscovery. As this differentiation became more clear, we explored the statistical relationships between the two types of problem cases. The patterns that emerged from both types of evaluation help explain the nature of the problems and their causes, and the relative efficacy of the present procedural rules in handling the two types of discovery problems.[9]

One difference was in who reported the case as having involved a discovery problem. All nine resistance cases were identified by plaintiffs' attorneys. Of the eleven overdiscovery cases, nine were identified by defendants' attorneys. Another difference was in the types of categories that seemed to describe the problems best. Although the subheadings used in chapter three were initially derived only for discussion purposes, they reveal interesting distinctions. For example, the subheadings under "Resistance to Discovery" in chapter three were "general resistance," "assertion of a privilege," "resisting document production," and "resisting answers to interrogatories." Except for the two cases that displayed a

---

9. The data presented in this chapter are descriptive statistics about the cases studied only. They are offered for their value in illustrating differences in these cases. The small number of cases studied and the extent of unexamined variables preclude any generalization of these observations to discovery problems in the wider world of civil cases. The relationships observed here, however, suggest the <u>possibility</u> of causal relationships. These possibilities should be kept in mind by case managers and by researchers who will continue to investigate discovery problems.

pattern of general resistance, resistance problems seemed to be related to the use of privilege or to the type of discovery device that had been used. Overdiscovery problems, on the other hand, did not seem related to the type of device. Instead, the type of case involved, the nature of the claim for relief, the nature of the evidence required, and the perceived degree of justification for the suit seemed to create natural groupings: expert testimony, novel theory, external causes, and claims that the defendant's attorney thought were groundless.

As noted in the beginning of chapter three, we originally divided the cases into those in which the discovery problem was based on a narrow or specific issue, those in which discovery problems were pervasive but which the reporting attorney did not characterize as involving a large volume of discovery, and those that had pervasive discovery problems and were described as having a large volume of discovery. Comparing the nine resistance cases with the eleven overdiscovery cases, we found that although four out of nine resistance cases were in the narrow-or-specific-issues group, and five in one of the two pervasive-problems groups, *all* of the overdiscovery cases involved pervasive discovery problems. In fact, all but one of the cases that we had originally categorized as large-volume, pervasive-problem cases were overdiscovery cases.

There were some differences in the types of cases in the resistance and overdiscovery categories, but the pattern of differences was not strong, possibly because the number of cases we studied was small. Most of the medical malpractice and contracts cases were in the overdiscovery category. There was one products liability case in each category. One distinguishing factor was that the two antitrust cases we studied were both reported to involve problems of overdiscovery.

The preceding differences between cases became apparent from our interviews with participants; we also collected data from case files and docket sheets and compared the resistance and overdiscovery cases based on those statistics.

TABLE 3

AVERAGE NUMBER OF DISCOVERY EVENTS

Discovery Event	Resistance Cases			Overdiscovery Cases		
	R[a]	O[b]	Both	R[a]	O[b]	Both
Sets of interrogatories	3.2	1.4	4.7	3.1	2.5	5.6
Requests for production	3.6	0.6	4.1	5.2	4.3	9.5
Depositions[c]	7.3	3.8	11.1	7.6	17.5	25.2
TOTAL	14.1	5.8	19.9	15.9	24.4	40.3

[a]Initiated by counsel reporting discovery problem.

[b]Initiated by opposing counsel.

[c]Includes only depositions filed with the court. Parties may have taken additional depositions and not filed them; these would not be reflected in our data. Each deposition filed, unless it was a continuation, was counted as a discovery event. We were unable to obtain an accurate count of depositions in two overdiscovery cases (the attorneys reported numerous depositions, but the records were unclear). Rather than eliminate all data pertaining to those two cases, we estimated the number of depositions in each of them as the average number of depositions initiated by the same party (reporting or opposing attorney) in the other overdiscovery cases. These estimates undoubtedly understated the actual number of depositions in the two cases.

Amount of Discovery

We measured the average amount of discovery in terms of the number of discovery events.[10] As shown in table 3, the average amount of dis-

---

10. A discovery event, as we are using the term here, consists of a deposition of an individual, a set of interrogatories, or a request for

covery in the overdiscovery cases was twice that in the resistance cases (40.3 events versus 19.9).[11] This difference is consistent with the perceptions of the reporting attorneys, even though it does not provide any evidence of the problems reported. The relationship generally holds true for each of the three major discovery devices, although there is less difference between the number of sets of interrogatories used than between the numbers of requests for production and depositions.

Distribution of Discovery Between Reporting and Opposing Counsel

In the resistance cases, counsel reporting the problem (the plaintiff's counsel in all the resistance cases) initiated more than twice as much discovery as the opposing counsel. In the overdiscovery cases, opposing counsel (those perceived as overdiscovering) did in fact initiate more total discovery events than the counsel reporting the problem, but that relationship was caused by differences in the number of depositions. Interrogatories and requests for production were used slightly more often by the reporting side. The data thus suggest that in the overdiscovery cases both sides were quite active in discovery.

---

production of documents. Although the use of other devices was recorded, the quantity was too small to reveal any patterns. If a discovery event was not filed with the court, it was not included in the data. The fact that an event occurred does not provide any clue to the amount of time it consumed. However, prior Center research confirms that counting events provides a reliable measure of the amount of discovery in a case. Connolly, Holleman, & Kuhlman, supra note 3, at 98.

11. Federal Judicial Center evaluation indicates that comparing the number of discovery events may understate the differences in cost and amount of time consumed by discovery. The time consumed by a deposition, the number of questions in a set of interrogatories, and the number of documents all tend to increase as the number of discovery events in a case increases. In statistical terms, there is a positive correlation between the number of discovery events in a case and the amount of time consumed by each event. P. Connolly & P. Lombard, Discovery Abuse: An Empirical Case Study (Fed. Judicial Center, forthcoming).

TABLE 4

AVERAGE ELAPSED TIME

	Resistance Cases	Overdiscovery Cases
Discovery	27.7 months	31.5 months
Case disposition	30.6 months	37.3 months

Amount of Time for Discovery and Case Disposition

The differences between volumes of discovery in the two categories might lead one to expect similar differences between the elapsed times for discovery and between the total times for case disposition. As shown in table 4, however, these differences were small, although in each instance overdiscovery cases took longer.

Motions to Compel Discovery

Table 5 shows the use of motions to compel discovery (rule 37(a)) in the two types of cases. Although the average number of rule 37(a) motions was the same for resistance and overdiscovery cases, there were differences in the distribution of motions between parties. For example, in the resistance cases, an average of 3.1 motions to compel were filed by reporting counsel (plaintiffs), compared to an average of only 0.4 by opposing counsel (defendants), or a ratio of approximately 8 to 1. This supports the reported perception of resistance. On the other hand, the ratio was more balanced in overdiscovery cases, indicating that discovery problems were more pervasive in those cases. It is of interest to note that although those cases were identified because of an overdiscovery problem, they also involved perceptions of resistance conduct on each side--reflected in the number of motions to compel.

The differences are also shown in terms of the rate of 37(a) motions; that is, the number of 37(a) motions per discovery event. The rate for resistance cases is twice that for overdiscovery cases. The difference is caused primarily by the large number of motions by reporting counsel (plaintiffs) in resistance cases. At a minimum, these data confirm their reported perceptions.

TABLE 5

MOTIONS TO COMPEL DISCOVERY

	Resistance Cases			Overdiscovery Cases		
	R[a]	O[b]	Both	R[a]	O[b]	Both
Average	3.1	0.4	3.6	1.9	1.6	3.5
Total	28	4	32	21	18	39
Granted	15 (54%)	1 (25%)	16 (50%)	7 (33%)	8 (44%)	15 (38%)
Number per discovery event	.220	.077	.179	.120	.067	.088

[a]Initiated by counsel reporting discovery problem.

[b]Initiated by opposing counsel.

As shown in table 5, there is a difference between the two categories in the percentage of 37(a) motions granted. On the average, 50 percent of all 37(a) motions were granted in the resistance cases. It is probably more important to note that 54 percent of the plaintifts' 37(a) motions were granted, which tends to validate the perception of the plaintiffs identifying those cases.[12] Only 38 percent of 37(a) motions were granted in the overdiscovery cases. That statistic may indicate that discovery was more complex and the need for it less certain in the overdiscovery cases, and that therefore the need for a motion to compel was less clear to the judge. The statistic may also indicate that a higher percentage of motions are mooted so that it is not necessary to grant the motion.

Motions for Protective Orders

Table 6 shows data on motions for protective orders under rule 26(c). As one might expect, defendants in the resistance cases moved for five times as many of these orders per case as did plaintiffs. That figure tends to confirm the resistance that plaintiffs perceived in most of these cases. The differences are less dramatic when the number of motions for protective orders is compared to the total number of opportunities (that is, the number of discovery events), but even on that basis the defendants' rate is twice as high as the plaintiffs'.

The number of motions for protective orders filed per overdiscovery case was only about one-third that per resistance case, and the rate of use of the motion was only one-sixth (.179 compared to .029).

Out of the relatively large number of defendants' motions for protective orders in the resistance cases, only slightly more than 7 percent were granted, again confirming the perception of resistance. The grant rate for resistance cases was 9 percent, while in the overdiscovery cases almost half the motions for protective orders were granted.

---

12. In the Federal Judicial Center's earlier discovery report, it was noted that 54% of the motions were granted. Connolly, Holleman, & Kuhlman, supra note 3, at 20 (table 6). However, that report indicated that only 59% of motions filed were ruled upon, resulting in a 92% grant rate for motions ruled upon. Assuming that the same ruling rate of 59% held true for this study, the 54% of motions granted in resistance cases may represent a 92% grant rate. When the data on percentage of motions granted in overdiscovery cases are adjusted in the same way, the grant rate becomes 66%.

TABLE 6

MOTIONS FOR PROTECTIVE ORDERS

	Resistance Cases			Overdiscovery Cases		
	R[a]	O[b]	Both	R[a]	O[b]	Both
Average	0.6	3.0	3.6	0.8	0.4	1.2
Total	5	27	32	9	4	13
Granted	1 (20%)	2 (7%)	3 (9%)	5 (56%)	1 (25%)	6 (46%)
Number per discovery event[c]	.096	.213	.179	.034	.023	.029

[a] Initiated by counsel reporting discovery problem.

[b] Initiated by opposing counsel.

[c] This rate is calculated by dividing the number of motions by the number of discovery events initiated by the opposition.

Motions for Sanctions

Table 7 shows the occurrence of motions for sanctions under rules 37(b) and (d). Resistance cases included an average of one such motion per case, all at the request of the plaintiff. Of the total nine motions for sanctions, six were granted. In contrast, the overdiscovery cases displayed a rate of motions for sanctions about one-third that of the resistance cases, or 0.3 per case. In fact, all three motions were in a single overdiscovery case; the nine motions in resistance cases were made in six different cases. The fact that the reporting attorneys did not file any 37(b) and (d) motions in overdiscovery cases could indicate that sanctions were not deemed useful in the overdiscovery cases or that the conduct complained about did not fit the requirements of rule 37.

TABLE 7

MOTIONS FOR SANCTIONS

	Resistance Cases			Overdiscovery Cases		
	R^a	O^b	Both	R^a	O^b	Both
Average	1	0	1	0	0.3	0.3
Total	9	0	9	0	3	3
Granted	6 (67%)	0	6 (67%)	0	3 (100%)	3 (100%)
Number per discovery event	.071	0	.050	0	.011	.007

[a] Initiated by counsel reporting discovery problem.

[b] Initiated by opposing counsel.

The use of motions for sanctions is probably better described by the number per discovery event. When the total number of discovery events is taken into account, as shown in table 7, the number of motions for sanctions per discovery event in resistance cases is about seven times that in the overdiscovery cases.

If rule 37(b) and (d) motions are an accurate indication of discovery abuse, one might infer that there is much less abuse in overdiscovery cases. However, the ratios shown above may indicate that overdiscovery problems reflect more substantive complexity than resistance problems, or that resistance is more easily measured and recognized because it is often related to quantifiable time periods or to specific events.

The Ad Damnum

Although one must be very cautious in using the amount of the prayer for damages (the ad damnum) to assess the importance of the matter at issue, gross differences in the amount of the prayer may help predict the size of the case and, in turn, the extent of the discovery as measured by cost and time. Of the nine resistance cases, seven had prayers for damages; the average amount was $1.1 million. Of the eleven overdiscovery cases, eight had prayers for damages, with an average amount of $18.2 million. This ratio of approximately sixteen to one[13] in the average ad damnum indicates there was substantially more money at issue in the overdiscovery cases.

The Number of Parties

The overdiscovery cases involved a larger average number of parties than the resistance cases, but the numbers were not substantially different. The average number of parties was 6.6 in overdiscovery cases, and 5.4 in resistance cases. The relationship between the number of parties plaintiff and parties defendant was approximately the same in each type of case, but the relative number of defendants in the overdiscovery cases was higher. In the overdiscovery cases, there were 5.2 defendants and 1.4 plaintiffs in the average case. In the resistance cases, there were 3.8 defendants and 1.6 plaintiffs in the average case.

---

13. In each category there was one case with an ad damnum substantially higher than that in the other cases. If data are skewed in this manner, one should compare the medians as well as the means (averages) to determine whether the same relationship exists. The ratio of the median ad damnums was about 11 to 1, which, although not quite as high as the mean ratio of 16 to 1, confirms a substantial difference between the two case categories.

VI. FACTORS AFFECTING DISCOVERY PROBLEMS

Most of the attorneys we interviewed mentioned factors that were not inherent in the cases themselves--factors that, in their opinion, contributed to the discovery problems they encountered. At the end of each interview, we asked the lawyers for their general opinions about the operation of the discovery rules in modern litigation. In the interviews and in perusals of case files, we observed other characteristics that appeared to be directly or indirectly related to particular discovery problems.

An exploration of these characteristics is necessary to a discussion of the types of remedial action needed to prevent discovery problems. If the causes of discovery problems lie in the rules, amendments would be appropriate. If the causes lie elsewhere, however, other types of action may be required, and attempts to prevent or correct problems through rule changes may be counterproductive.

Because it includes only those factors that emerged from the twenty-three cases we studied, the list of characteristics presented in this chapter may represent only a portion of the elements that affect discovery problems. Nor can conclusions be drawn from this study about the relative importance of each factor or the frequency with which it affects cases. Even so, the list suggests that the sources of problems are broad in subject and myriad in number, in contrast to past reports that have pointed to narrow aspects of the rules themselves as the primary (and implicitly, sole) causes of discovery problems.

The Parties and Their Relationship

Relative Resources of Parties

The relative resources of the parties seemed to be related to discovery problems in several of the cases. Our study of resistance cases in which the economic strength of parties differed substantially indicated that the amount and duration of the resistance were greater than would be expected from the discovery issues involved. In two of the overdiscovery cases, the reporting attorneys believed that the greater economic strength of the opposing party was a major factor in explaining the overdiscovery.

The federal government was the resisting party in one case and an overdiscovering party in another. In each instance, the government's lack of incentive to conserve costs and its substantial resources were cited as causal factors in discovery problems.

The effect of parties' ill-matched resources is perhaps best illustrated by one attorney's statement that his "client will think long and hard before going to court against a giant company again."

Motive for Bringing Suit or Defending an Action

In several cases, the motivation for bringing suit seemed to be directly related to the plaintiff's going out of business. In some instances the plaintiff's major asset appeared to be a cause of action that might ultimately provide money. In one case, the defunct plaintiff corporation took the position that it had been driven out of business by the defendant's illegal acts. It was quite clear that the defense attorneys saw suits of this type as groundless; in assessing the degree of discovery, they had difficulty separating their feelings about the motivation for the suit from their perception about the amount of discovery in the case. In each instance that involved this type of motive, the defendant's attorney reported the case as involving overdiscovery.

Animosity Between the Parties

Animosity between the parties existed in several cases. In some instances that feeling might have precipitated the actual filing of the suit. Animosity clearly affected the perception of resistance to discovery or overdiscovery, and it seemed to create or exacerbate discovery problems. When animosity was reported as being a cause of the problem (or appeared to be so), and when we were able to discuss it with the judge in the case, its role as a cause was confirmed. In one instance, the judge noted that the parties had been enemies in politics and business and that they had brought their enmity to a new forum. In another case where enmity between the parties existed, the judge agreed with the defendant's attorney that the suit was probably frivolous, but that his throwing it out of court would have been reversed by the court of appeals. In other cases the judges believed that animosity between parties did not affect the amount of discovery, but did increase the general level of contentiousness, leading to more hearings and a greater total cost of discovery, both to the litigants and to the court system.

Substantial Interest Beyond the Claim Itself

Sometimes filing a lawsuit is only part of an overall strategy or program, such as a public interest group's efforts to effect change. The program may include legislative initiatives and projects aimed at educating, informing, and persuading the electorate. Litigation, when it becomes part of the strategy, is not an end in itself, but it has specific objectives as part of the larger effort. In such cases, this strategy will affect discovery as well as the perceptions of the opposing attorneys. In at least one case of this type, the suit was clearly part of a larger plan. In some other cases that involved public interest representation, however, the filing of the suit seemed to have a clear and singular purpose, seeking a specific remedy (money damages) for a specific injury. In those cases, it appeared that the defendants were reacting to what they perceived as a larger strategy (which may or may not have existed). Their perception of the opponent's purposes and strategy seemed to have a strong influence on their course of discovery, particularly on the amount of resistance they offered.

Multiple Parties

Our data showed a clear relationship between the number of parties in a case and the amount of discovery. Of the cases we studied, those with more parties involved more discovery. This relationship occurred regardless of the nature of the claim for relief. Data on the number of parties showed that the overdiscovery cases had an average of 25 percent more parties than the resistance cases, thus confirming our observation.

The extent to which increasing the number of parties results in more discovery is strongly affected by whether the interests--especially of defendants--are separable. For instance, in a medical malpractice case in which several doctors were defendants, separability of interests resulted in separate experts for each defendant and a resulting increase in the amount of discovery.

The Attorneys and the Law Firms

Comparative Experience of Opposing Attorneys

One attorney stated that openness of document discovery is a function of the lawyer's experience and competence. In several instances, experienced attorneys complained that the problem of overdiscovery stemmed from young lawyers' inexperience. The young attorneys, they said, are not able to cut to the heart of the matter and are afraid to overlook anything. Furthermore, they added, the inexperienced lawyers are inefficient in conducting depositions and often do not know exactly what they are looking for. Several experienced lawyers said that this inefficiency was the cause of extremely long depositions, of interrogatories with large numbers of subparts, and of overly broad requests for production of documents.

One could speculate that because discovery constitutes one of the major costs in litigation, attorneys' inexperience and lack of advocacy skills cost the system much more in pretrial phases than in the relatively small percentage of cases that actually go to trial. Therefore, perhaps younger attorneys should receive more training in direct examination and cross-examination. As one attorney stated, "It's very difficult to do a proper job of discovery until one has had some experience." Another attorney made the point more forcefully, saying that "inexperience always results in excessive or wasteful discovery."

Comparative Degree of Specialization

The relative degree of opposing attorneys' specialization seemed to have a very important effect on their perception of resistance to discovery or of overdiscovery. As might be expected, we observed more of this specialization on the defense side. Defense attorneys whose practices were relatively specialized tended to view askance the approach of plaintiffs' attorneys with less expertise. Their perceptions, especially concerning what they deemed overdiscovery, seemed to be influenced by their attitude that they were specialists viewing nonspecialists.

Specialization has two aspects: knowledge of and experience with substantive areas of law (e.g., antitrust, products liability, etc.) and knowledge of and experience with the subject of the case (e.g., the type of business or the type of injury). When opposing attorneys were both specialists in an area of law, but one was also familiar with the particular business involved in the case, the two lawyers differed noticeably in their approach to and perceptions of discovery. A less knowledgeable lawyer might use discovery as a method for learning about the business, which his more knowledgeable opponent might view as excessive discovery. Not only might the nonspecialist tend to seek extensive discovery, but he also might be taken advantage of by a more experienced opponent whose greater familiarity with the matter enables him to delay or obfuscate discovery.

We noticed that in cases involving several different theories, the discovering lawyer would give priority to the area with which he was most familiar. Often, the opposing lawyer thought the chosen emphasis was irrelevant. In two instances, opposing attorneys who were interviewed pointed to that approach as a cause of unnecessary and excessive discovery.

Protection Against Legal Malpractice Claims

In some of the cases reported as instances of overdiscovery, the reporting attorneys later postulated that some overdiscovery resulted from opposing counsel's concern to protect themselves against malpractice claims by following a strategy designed to "leave no stone unturned." Two attorneys noted a recent trend towards conducting discovery as protection against possible malpractice claims.

We observed this strategy occurring primarily on the part of plaintiffs' attorneys, and more in tort cases--especially medical malpractice and products liability cases--than in contract or statutory actions. The phenomenon is less noticeable in a contract case because the difficulty usually stems at least partially from the activity of other lawyers--those who wrote and negotiated the contract. In a tort case, the plaintiff's attorney is the only one the client can hold responsible if the outcome is not to his liking. And when an attorney is prosecuting a medical malpractice case, the issue of professional liability--including his own performance in the case--necessarily pervades his thinking.

Comparative Attorney Styles

Differences in attorneys' styles always affected the lawyers' perceptions of discovery and sometimes were the cause of discovery problems. Some attorneys, for example, rarely use depositions and conduct almost all of their discovery through interrogatories and requests for production, while others consider interrogatories to be of limited use and view depositions as the best discovery device.

In some instances the choice of discovery devices seemed to be more dependent on style than on the individual characteristics of the case. None of the young attorneys in the cases we studied favored interrogatories and requests for production over depositions. The attorneys who emphasized that approach were all senior attorneys. Attorneys who used mainly interrogatories and requests for production did conduct less discovery over all, and they were more likely to perceive discovery by the opponent--who used a different style--as excessive, even when the judge in the case did not view it that way.

There were also noticeable differences in attorneys' degree of aggressiveness and persistence in pursuing discovery. In some resistance cases, the perception of resistance was clearly affected by the aggressiveness and persistence of the reporting attorney. Objectively measurable delay was clearly occurring, but the threshold for determining when delay became resistance was clearly correlated with style. In one case, a judge who had granted a plaintiff's motion to compel discovery emphasized that although he had granted the motion, the primary cause of discovery problems in the case was the attitude and style of the plaintiff's attorney.

Attorneys use different approaches in responding to interrogatories they feel are irrelevant or improper. Some attorneys object; others deal with the problem by entering responses such as "not applicable" or "see records." We observed the latter approach primarily in cases where boilerplate interrogatories had been used.

Acrimony Between the Attorneys

We observed less acrimony between lawyers than animosity between parties. Where it did exist, however, it obviously affected the perception of resistance to discovery or overdiscovery. Further, it made discovery more troublesome and prone to problems. In one case, the judge attributed all the discovery problems to one attorney's personality and approach, which, he said, "could not fail to create instant acrimony" between that attorney and his opponent. According to the judge, that was the discovery problem--not what appeared on the docket sheet and in the documents supporting discovery motions.

In one case, the judge pointed out that there was considerable resentment between an attorney for one party and the representative of the opposing party (an organization). He felt that this bitterness had some effect on discovery in the case and that it created problems at trial. He was unable to relate this acrimony to either resistance or overdiscovery in the case, but he did feel that it affected the attorneys' perception.

Acquaintance of the Opposing Attorneys

Previous research has confirmed that among members of a close-knit bar--close-knit because of specialty or because the lawyers are in a small, nonurban area--there is often less formal discovery than in other cases.[14] The moderation of formal discovery and the importance of the long-term relationships among the attorneys lead to fewer discovery problems. In most of the cases we studied, opposing attorneys did not know each other well. This unfamiliarity may have given rise to discovery problems of both types--resistance and overdiscovery. Our observations are therefore not surprising: we examined only problem cases and we found little familiarity between opposing counsel.

One should not infer, however, that if attorneys know each other there will be no discovery problems. That did appear to be true in resistance cases, but in two overdiscovery cases the opposing attorneys knew each other well, having worked together before. Plaintiffs' counsel stated there was mutual respect and a good working relationship between the respective attorneys and their firms, but the cases were complex, with many issues to be explored through discovery. One can only surmise that the problems might have been exacerbated if the attorneys had not been acquainted.

The likelihood of opposing attorneys' being future adversaries is closely related to familiarity and may also contribute to cooperation, or at least to reduced contentiousness. We did not encounter any cases in which attorneys might have expected to meet in future litigation, as might have been the case in a nonurban area or in litigation that tends to involve close-knit, specialized bars, such as patent, copyright, or admiralty actions. Again, our finding is not surprising because we studied only cases with discovery problems.

Relative Size of Law Firms

Discovery problems sometimes arose when a sole practitioner or a member of a two-, three-, or four-person firm faced an opposing attorney

---

14. Connolly, Holleman, & Kuhlman, supra note 3, at 97-98.

from a large firm. Law firm size itself did not seem to significantly affect discovery problems for firms larger than that size. In fact, one attorney from a small firm who reported a case in which another small firm had resisted discovery, noted that "large firms that have had experience don't obfuscate." Although this study involved too few cases on which to base quantitative distinctions, we observed that once law firm size reached ten attorneys, size did not seem to have any clear effect.

Comparative Law Firm Styles

Just as individual styles differ, law firms have distinguishable institutional styles that vary from firm to firm. In several cases, this factor seemed to affect the lawyers' perceptions as well as the discovery problems. One style that was used in several cases was assigning a phalanx of attorneys to the case and hitting the other side with a barrage of discovery, making them feel that a major assault was under way. The opposing attorneys reacted with surprise, especially if their firms' styles were different. There did not seem to be a strong relationship between this practice and the size of the matter at issue. Rather, the "barrage approach" seemed to be the style adopted by some large firms. Because large firms often handle cases involving large amounts of money or issues of great importance to the parties, the style becomes a standard practice, applied in most cases.

We also observed some differences in the degree to which law firms obtained information through formal discovery devices, through informal devices, or through investigators. In one case, more than 90 percent of the information that one firm obtained during the discovery period was developed by investigators and paralegals conducting market surveys; on the other side, all of the information was obtained through formal discovery. In cases that displayed this difference, the party using informal methods saw the opponent's discovery as excessive.

The Attorney's Relationship to the Client

The Attorney's Control Over the Case

Our judicial system relies on attorneys to control discovery, which in turn depends on lawyers' having full authority to act. However, the attorney's usual authority may have to be shared if the client has special concerns, such as professional reputation, institutional survival, or a strongly felt position. Counsel's authority may also be affected if a client has in-house lawyers and retains additional, outside attorneys.

The attorneys' degree of control over the cases we studied was clearly related to discovery problems, both in resistance and in overdiscovery cases. When a party had strong feelings about the matter at issue, the attorney apparently had more difficulty in controlling the course of discovery, regardless of whether the problem involved resistance or overdiscovery. In at least one instance, the case changed dramatically once the attorneys were able to convince their client to accept their professional advice. In some other instances, lack of control throughout the case seemed to be associated with discovery problems.

Direct Contact Between Attorney and Client

Attorney-client contact is closely related to the attorney's control over a case. If access is limited, the usual authority of the lawyer is also limited. The effect appeared most clearly in two types of cases we studied: those with insurance company representation, and those that involved a government agency. In several cases, attorneys had to work through insurance adjustors and did not have direct contact with their clients. In at least two instances that situation seemed to be the primary cause of the perceived resistance. In one case it resulted in a large recovery of attorney expenses. Cases in which a state or federal government agency was a party presented problems because the attorney representing the non-government party had to deal with an attorney whose organization was at least once removed from the organization that was the actual party in the case. The resulting communication and coordination problems were not usually encountered when a private party was involved, except for those instances in which insurance company representation was used. In at least two cases that involved insurance company representation, problems arose from the restrictions that the insurance company placed on the attorney. These restrictions reduced the attorney's authority and his control over the case, and led directly to discovery problems and increased costs.

Organizational Problems in Coordinating Responses

Delays in responses to discovery were sometimes related to problems of coordination among several entities who were named parties in a case. One example was a case in which a corporation and one of its subsidiaries were defendants. Both entities had discoverable documents and officers who were subject to being deposed or responding to interrogatories. Discovery problems occurred when no one within the corporate hierarchy took command to coordinate the litigation, a task that would normally fall to the general counsel's office. This type of problem made it difficult for the attorney representing these parties to coordinate discovery responses in a timely manner, even though the attorney may have had direct contact with both the subsidiary and its parent.

The Fee Arrangement

Whether an attorney is working for an hourly fee or a contingent fee would seem to be a factor in the conduct of discovery. We observed that plaintiffs' attorneys who were working on a contingent fee basis were more sensitive to resistance to discovery--a logical sensitivity, because resistance by the other party increases cost to the discoverer. However, hourly billing arrangements did not seem to affect plaintiffs' attorneys' perceptions of overdiscovery by the other party. That is, although the extra time required by an opponent's overdiscovery would result in more billable hours, the attorneys did not display a "pocketbook reaction." They felt the system was being misused, and the fact that they would benefit financially from the misuse did not affect their perception.

Thus, although fee arrangement would seem to affect the amount of discovery in a case, the cases in this study did not support that conclusion. Attorneys working on hourly and contingent fee bases expressed the same degree of concern about the cost of discovery. It should be noted that our observations apply only to attorneys' perceptions of discovery. We did not have data to determine whether there is actually any relationship between the amount of discovery and the fee arrangement.

The Judge and Judicial Procedures

The Judge's Knowledge and Experience

None of the attorneys we interviewed reported that the judge's knowledge and experience with the type of case at issue affected discovery problems, although several mentioned the lack of time the judge spent on the case (see below). One of the judges we interviewed raised this issue, however. He noted, for example, that his district gets very few antitrust cases, and his relative unfamiliarity makes him more hesitant to control the scope of discovery in antitrust actions. He thought that judges in districts where many such cases are filed should be able to control discovery better and to know when dismissal or summary judgment is appropriate. He added that judges who had tried such cases when they were attorneys, or who had received specialized training, would similarly be better able to control discovery.

Extent of Judicial Control and Early Involvement

The relationship between judicial control procedures and discovery was mentioned by twelve of the initial interviewees for the twenty-three cases in this study. That relationship was mentioned more often than any other factor affecting discovery. It was mentioned in six of the eleven overdiscovery cases, four of the nine resistance cases, and two of the three cases that were reported to involve a single or isolated problem.

In one overdiscovery case, in which discovery took three years, the reporting attorney asserted that the amount of discovery could have been reduced substantially and the case could have gone to trial in one year if the judge had used stricter control procedures. In another overdiscovery case, the reporting attorney complained that the judge did not take control until the very end of the case. He implied that if the judge had taken control early, there would have been substantially less discovery. In another case involving a single instance of overdiscovery, the reporting attorney complained that the judge knew nothing about the case and did not want to listen to details, instead instructing the lawyer to give the other party everything they asked for. He opined that this type of judicial response was one cause of unnecessary discovery costs. In one resistance case, the reporting attorney noted that the judge "was not active in the case." He felt the judge's active involvement would have resolved or precluded most of the resistance in that case.

We asked the reporting attorneys in two overdiscovery cases whether an early discovery conference, such as is envisioned in the proposed new subsection (f) of rule 26,[15] would have prevented the problems in their

---

15. The proposed subsection (f), which was approved by the Judicial Conference of the United States in September, 1979, is as follows:

(f) Discovery Conference. At any time after commencement of an action the court may direct the attorneys for the parties to appear before it for a conference on the subject of discovery. The court shall do so upon motion by the attorney for any party if the motion includes:
    (1) A statement of the issues as they then appear;
    (2) A proposed plan and schedule of discovery;
    (3) Any limitations proposed to be placed on discovery;
    (4) Any other proposed orders with respect to discovery; and
    (5) A statement showing that the attorney making the motion
has made a reasonable effort to reach agreement with opposing attorneys on the matters set forth in the motion. Each party and his attorney are under a duty to participate in good faith in the framing of a discovery plan if a plan is proposed by the attorney for any party. Notice of the motion shall be served on all parties. Objections or additions to matters set forth in the motion shall be served not later than 10 days after service of the motion.

Following the discovery conference, the court shall enter an order tentatively identifying the issues for discovery purposes, establishing a

cases. One responded that he doubted the case could have been narrowed early in the proceedings unless the judge had spent a lot of time on it. Although he thought it would be highly desirable for judges to spend the amount of time required to conduct such conferences, he noted that the present caseload of federal judges might impede time-consuming involvement. In the second case in which we posed this question, the attorney said that he would not have asked for a discovery conference early in the case because initially, he thought the case was a simple one. With hindsight, he believed that a discovery conference to narrow the issues would have been helpful.

In two cases, counsel viewed the court's refusal to limit discovery as contributing to a large amount of unnecessary discovery. In the first case, the judge refused counsel's request to limit the number of witnesses listed by the opposing party. The reporting attorney believed that such a limitation would have helped to minimize the potential for discovery abuse by opposing counsel. In the second case--one involving a novel theory--the attorney felt that the judge was being overly cautious; the judge was reluctant to restrict discovery because it might deprive a party of potentially important information. That case, according to the reporting attorney, involved an "outrageous" amount of discovery by both sides.

In three of the four resistance cases in which judicial control was mentioned, positive comments were made. In one case, the reporting attorney said that the judge kept tight control over every phase of discovery, which reduced costs as well as providing a fairer trial. In another

---

plan and schedule for discovery, setting limitations on discovery, if any; and determining such other matters, including the allocation of expenses, as are necessary for the proper management of discovery in the action. An order may be altered or amended whenever justice so requires.

Subject to the right of a party who properly moves for a discovery conference to prompt convening of the conference, the court may combine the discovery conference with a pretrial conference authorized by Rule 16.

case, the attorney noted that although no early conference was held, the judge ruled quickly on all motions and thus solved the resistance problem in every instance. A third attorney noted that judicial control had not been a problem in his case and emphasized that whether the rules work depends to a large extent on the judge.

In contrast to the generally positive tone of comments about judicial control in resistance cases, the comments were negative in all of the overdiscovery cases where judicial control was mentioned. The attorneys reporting those cases felt there was insufficient or inadequate judicial control, and that it was strongly related to the overdiscovery problem.

Judicial control was mentioned in two of the three cases involving an isolated or single occurrence of misuse or abuse. In one case, the problem was attributed to judicial attitude; in the other, the judge's active involvement solved the problem quickly.

The pattern that emerges from these comments is one of generally favorable reaction to the effects of judicial control and to the type of judicial control exercised in the resistance cases, and generally unfavorable reaction to the judicial control exercised in the overdiscovery cases. Every attorney who mentioned judicial control in overdiscovery cases perceived lack of control as contributing to the discovery problems; they felt that better judicial control could have precluded or corrected the problems.

The nature of control procedures and the extent to which a judge spends time on a case in its early stages is sometimes more important than the mere fact of judicial control or the lack of it. For example, in one overdiscovery case, the reporting attorney noted that there had been four status conferences, but that none of them had helped. He said the only thing that did seem to help was setting a trial date, although that merely accelerated the pace of discovery without decreasing the amount. In his opinion, if the judge had become more actively involved and had learned more about the case, the amount of discovery could have been reduced substantially. In accord with the attorney's observation in this case, prior Center research showed that reductions in the elapsed time for discovery do not require the judge's active involvement or extensive expenditure of time and that reductions in elapsed time do not affect the amount of discovery.[16]

The extent to which a judge is able to learn the details of a case during discovery may also be related to the extent to which sanctions are imposed. Several attorneys complained that most judges are reluctant to "get tough" and invoke sanctions when the discovery process is abused. One attorney asserted that this reluctance is a direct result of judicial unwillingness to get involved in the details of discovery. In his opinion, because judges refrain from involvement in discovery, they are not sufficiently familiar with the case and are therefore hesitant to impose severe sanctions such as expenses, exclusion, or default.

Case Characteristics

The Timing of the Decision to Sue

In two cases that defense counsel perceived as being overdiscovered, the complaint was hurriedly filed to fall within the statute of limitations. This haste may have affected the amount of formal discovery conducted by the plaintiffs. When the prospective plaintiffs consulted counsel about bringing suit, little time remained in which to file the complaint, and pre-filing, informal discovery was simply not possible. The informal discovery that normally would have taken place before a complaint was filed had to be completed after filing, and formal discovery devices were used to obtain information. Also, because the complaints were drafted quickly, they were somewhat less precise than they might otherwise have been. The lack of precision and relatively greater use of formal discovery led to defense counsel's perception of duplicative and unnecessary discovery.

---

16. Connolly, Holleman, & Kuhlman, supra note 3, at 59.

The Claim for Relief

Most of the cases in this study that involved narrow or specific discovery problems were based upon a transaction. When the claim for relief was based on a course of conduct, however, as in an antitrust suit, a fraud action, or Title VII litigation, the case was almost always one that was reported to involve pervasive overdiscovery. In most of these cases, the amount of discovery seemed directly related to the nontransactional, broad nature of the claim for relief. Cases of this type also sometimes involve the need to prove motive and intent, and this in itself usually requires more discovery than a case based upon an accident or a breach of contract. And if the facts are all in the hands of the defendant, as is true in some cases of this type, there is a tendency to discover more than might otherwise be necessary.

Frivolous Claims

It is difficult to decide, even with hindsight, whether a claim is frivolous. Defense attorneys in several of the overdiscovery cases insinuated that the cases were frivolous. Yet of the six overdiscovery cases that were tried, the plaintiffs prevailed in two. In one of these cases we had left the initial interview with the impression that the plaintiff had lost. Later, a review of the court files showed that the judge had ruled in the plaintiff's favor.

In one overdiscovery case, the judge agreed with the defendant's attorney that the claim had been frivolous and that it was "the grossest abuse of the discovery process" he had ever seen. It was only after considerable discovery and preparation of a pretrial order, however, that it became clear the plaintiff had no case. Thus, although a frivolous claim clearly leads to wasteful discovery, the determination of frivolity was not an easy matter in any of the cases in this study.

Novel Theory

In several cases in which a novel theory was essential to the plaintiff's claim for relief, extensive discovery was required to develop the theory, and the defense counsel perceived the discovery as disproportionate. In each case where this occurred, the judge confirmed the importance of the novel theory as the cause of the problem.

Counterclaims

The cases in which defendants filed counterclaims involved substantially more discovery than would otherwise have been conducted--and a higher level of contentiousness. This observation is supported by prior Center research indicating that a counterclaim generates approximately as much discovery as the original complaint.[17]

Expert Testimony

When expert testimony is central to a case, often at least one party perceives overdiscovery. In several instances, expert testimony created problems for the plaintiff and required extensive discovery on his part.

The effect of expert testimony on discovery problems was especially evident in medical malpractice cases and in one of the products liability cases. In these types of cases, expert testimony is often critical in establishing the liability of the defendant. The need for a favorable expert increases the likelihood of counsel's "shopping" for one whose testimony will withstand cross-examination by the opposing party. In one of the malpractice cases, the plaintiff's attorney reported that he deposed seven or eight expert witnesses listed by the defendant--only two of whom were eventually called at the trial. He believed that the depositions had rendered the other experts useless to the defendant. The use of experts, therefore, can entail trial-and-error discovery or, as reported to us, overdiscovery.

Locating a favorable expert during the discovery period may not always be possible. In three overdiscovery cases in which discovery took

---

17. Connolly, Holleman, & Kuhlman, supra note 3, at 47.

more than two-and-a-half years, the plaintiff in each case did not locate a favorable expert witness until two or three weeks before trial.

In one case we observed what appeared to be an abuse of the rules. On three occasions in this case, the defendant's counsel listed as a witness an individual whom the plaintiff's attorney then deposed. After the plaintiff's deposition of that person, the defense counsel listed the same person as an expert witness. The plaintiff's counsel felt that this required a second deposition of these individuals and increased discovery costs.

The Ad Damnum

Because we studied only problem cases, rather than a random sample of all cases, we cannot infer any relationship between the size of the <u>ad damnum</u> and the existence of discovery problems. Further, such information would not provide insight into factors that affect discovery in cases seeking nonmonetary relief. However, our data comparing the average <u>ad damnum</u> in resistance cases with that in overdiscovery cases indicate that the average <u>ad damnum</u> in the latter is sixteen times that in the former. From these data, one might infer that a larger <u>ad damnum</u> is likely to result in a larger amount of discovery (which may be perceived as overdiscovery).

In several cases, the absolute size of the potential liability was an important factor in the defendant's extensive discovery, which the plaintiff's counsel perceived as overdiscovery.

Peripheral Participants

In two resistance cases, attorneys reported that one cause of the discovery problems they encountered was the lack of knowledge and experience of insurance adjustors who were handling responses to requests for production of documents. One attorney said adjustors typically report that documents do not exist when in fact they do exist. The other attorney said that the lack of understanding about the discovery process on the part of adjustors who were serving as liaisons greatly exacerbated the resistance he encountered.

The Rules of Civil Procedure

One of the objectives of this study was to examine how the rules of civil procedure are operating and the extent to which rules themselves may cause discovery problems. If serious problems exist in the rules, one could expect that attorneys would have reported one or more rules, or parts of them, as the cause of a discovery problem. However, even if attorneys did not name rules as causes of problems, one should not assume that the rules are problem-free.

In order to assure that we did not overlook any problems that might exist in the rules themselves, we asked each attorney whether the occurrence of the problem he reported could be precluded in the future by a rule change. All but one of the comments we heard about the rules were made in response to that question.[18] Most of the attorneys responded in the negative. Several, however, had suggestions for changes in the rules.

One defense attorney, reporting an overdiscovery case that he considered groundless, thought there should be arbitrary time limits on depositions and limits on the number of depositions and interrogatories. Several other attorneys agreed that arbitrary limits on the amount of discovery (with additional discovery by leave of court) were both feasible and desirable. One attorney felt that eliminating the term "subject matter" in rule 26(b)(1) and replacing it with "issues" would prevent overdiscovery problems. However, the response from attorneys reporting overdiscovery problems was exemplified by one attorney who, in responding

---

18. The one exception was a case in which overdiscovery had occurred--according to the defendant's attorney--because the plaintiff had proceeded on a general defect theory. One could interpret the attorney's statement as an implicit criticism of the scope of discovery allowed under rule 26(b)(1). On the other hand, one could also argue that the case was a perfect example of the modern pleading process. Although the judge allowed discovery on the general defect theory, he would not let the case go to the jury unless a specific defect was alleged. The discovery process led to revelation of the specific defect that was introduced as evidence at trial.

to the question of whether the excessive discovery he reported could be corrected by a rule change, stated, "Rule changes couldn't affect this! This [overdiscovery] is controlled by the individual abilities and integrity of attorneys--this is what governs whether or not abuse occurs." Another experienced lawyer gave a broader answer: "There's no way to cut down discovery as long as there are fertile brains in the profession."

The responses of attorneys reporting resistance problems were more detailed. The single most repeated complaint was that the rules were not being adequately enforced. One attorney stated generally that "tough" enforcement of the rules would eliminate resistance problems. Several others focused on the granting of expenses when a rule 37(a) motion to compel discovery is granted. Five attorneys reported the number of rule 37(a) motions they had filed requesting expenses. Only one motion for expenses had been granted. If the attorneys' estimates are accurate, their collective experience was that only one out of about 250 such motions was granted. One attorney felt that "there should be an almost automatic award of expenses under rule 37(a) motions." Another, who had emphasized that "there should be a remedy for dilatory tactics in responding to discovery requests," added that "there should be severe sanctions which a judge could impose sua sponte."

Attorneys reporting problems of resistance to discovery suggested other specific rule changes. One lawyer felt that rule 33 should be strengthened to assure that answers to interrogatories are signed by the person making them. In the case he reported, insurance company counsel had prepared unsigned, unsworn, and undated answers to interrogatories that, at trial, turned out to be false. The reporting attorney said that when a corporation is the party answering interrogatories, only persons with personal knowledge of the facts should answer. For example, if the questions concern product testing, the person in charge of the tests should answer for the corporation.

Another attorney was critical of rule 30(b)(6) as it works in practice. He said that in many cases the deposing attorney does not know the designation of the person to testify on behalf of an organization until the time of the deposition. This attorney thought that the rule should require designation in writing, in advance. Further, the designee should be someone who has personal knowledge of the matters about which he will testify; the subjects about which he will testify should be designated (the rule presently says the deponent "may set forth" the subjects); and the designee's expertise should be described.

Two attorneys emphasized the need for improvement in rule 34, especially to cover situations in which rule 34 requests are handled by claims agents through an attorney retained by an insurer. In each instance where that method was reported, the claims agents were not familiar with the documents of the insured parties and did not seem to positively ensure that a knowledgeable person would prepare, supervise, or coordinate the response. The reporting attorneys felt there should be a better method for making certain that the party, not an intermediary, responds. One attorney reported that the typical response to rule 34 requests, signed by claims agents, is "we don't have any." He asserted that in many instances this response turns out to be incorrect.

VII. CONCLUSIONS AND RECOMMENDATIONS

Conclusions

Every practitioner and judge knows that discovery problems stem from a number of sources. Yet, when solutions are discussed, there has been a tendency to focus on one or two narrow changes as remedies. An example of this tendency was the position taken by the Litigation Section of the American Bar Association: that if the term "subject matter" in rule 26(b)(1) were either deleted or changed to "issues," and if more sanctions were made available and used, overdiscovery problems would be eliminated.

Neither of these changes would affect most of the factors that cause discovery problems. Our review of factors affecting discovery, although limited because we studied a small number of problem cases, indicates that there are myriad causes, many of which are not subject to direct control by either rules or judges. The discovery rules cannot prevent such factors as differing attorney styles, relative law firm size, acrimony between attorneys or parties, motives for bringing suit, or the relative resources of the parties from causing discovery problems. Rules could be promulgated to cover experience and specialization, but those factors involve policy concerns far broader than discovery, and discovery problems alone would not seem to justify such rules.

The identification of a multiplicity of factors affecting discovery problems leads to several conclusions. First, and most obviously, discovery problems cannot be addressed through any single solution such as a change in a rule. Second, many of the causal factors arise out of the adversary system itself. Third, many of the factors are related to major changes in procedural and substantive law over the past several decades. Fourth, the judge's awareness of the existence of these factors early in a case holds the potential for adequately handling many discovery problems. Judges cannot (and should not) directly control most of the factors that can contribute to discovery problems. They are, however, in a position to control and mitigate the effects of those factors. In some cases this can prevent the occurrence of problems; in others, it can lead to timely and effective solutions.

Differences Between Resistance and Overdiscovery Cases

Perhaps the most significant result of our study was the identification of major differences between cases with resistance problems and cases with overdiscovery problems. These differences began to appear during our initial interviews. Resistance problems were related more to the type of discovery device being used when the problem occurred, while overdiscovery problems were more closely related to the nature of the claim for relief, the nature of the evidence required, or the basis for the claim. Overdiscovery problems were to some extent inherent in substantive matters, while resistance problems came more often from sources not inherent in the substance of the case. In turn, resistance problems were relatively narrow and specific, while overdiscovery problems were more pervasive.

Our identification of factors that can cause, exacerbate, or prolong discovery problems was not the result of a rigorous analytical process, and caution is warranted in drawing inferences about the strength or frequency of occurrence of any factor. Yet it is interesting to note that more of the factors were related to overdiscovery than to resistance problems. Although this difference may have arisen because some factors that lead to resistance were simply not identified in the cases studied, it may indicate more potential for the occurrence of overdiscovery problems.

Further differences emerged among attorneys' comments about the extent to which a rule had caused a discovery problem and whether a change in the rules would preclude the occurrence of the problem in the future. Attorneys reporting resistance cases gave more particular responses and more suggestions for rules changes. Several attorneys reporting resistance cases felt that more stringent enforcement of existing rules would both prevent and solve resistance problems. In contrast, attorneys reporting overdiscovery cases more often responded that rules changes would not affect overdiscovery problems. The two suggestions for rules changes to affect overdiscovery (see below) were more significant in terms of potential impact, however, perhaps reflecting the seriousness of the problem.

Differences between the two types of cases continued to appear when we examined the issue of judicial control. Judicial control was mentioned by attorneys in four resistance cases. In two of these, the attorney stated that the judge's quick, effective action had solved the resistance problem; in a third case, the attorney reported that control had been adequate. In the fourth case, the attorney felt a more active posture on the judge's part had been needed. In contrast to the positive reaction of three attorneys reporting resistance cases, all six attorneys reporting overdiscovery problems who mentioned judicial control felt there had been insufficient and inadequate judicial control in the cases they reported. They believed that this lack of control had contributed to the problem. Further, they all felt that stronger control and earlier involvement by the judge would have prevented some problems and would have served to correct problems that did occur.

Our review of case files and docket sheets confirmed the existence of differences between resistance and overdiscovery cases and revealed other characteristics that distinguished the two categories. Cases in which the lawyers identified overdiscovery problems more often involved multiple parties, included greater use of depositions, and indeed had twice as much discovery as cases in which the problem turned on resistance. The implicit suggestion that overdiscovery problems were associated with size and complexity was strengthened when we observed that the <u>ad damnum</u> tended to be far higher than in the resistance cases. Conversely, relatively little of this heightened discovery activity was subjected to motions for rule 37 sanction. At least in the cases studied, then, the activities of the lawyers accorded with the view they expressed about the potential effects of rule enforcement.

All these differences suggest several conclusions. It seems clear that rule-makers and judges must recognize that different responses are required for the two types of problems. It also seems clear that we are dealing here with more than differences in discovery. In fact, the discovery differences are merely symptoms and manifestations of deeper, more substantial underlying differences in the types of cases and situations that give rise to the two different types of problems.

Differences in Solutions

Just as there are differences between overdiscovery and resistance problems and the types of cases in which they occur, there are differences in the solutions available for these problems. The existing rules seem to provide sufficient mechanisms to control extremes and abuses related to resistance. But they do not contain adequate mechanisms to deal with the extremes and abuses of overdiscovery, and it is not clear that such mechanisms could easily be developed in rule form. An exception to this conclusion might be rules setting arbitrary limits on the amount of discovery that could be conducted without leave of court. However, defining a measure to determine the threshold level for court intervention presents its own difficulties. Several districts are experimenting with limits on interrogatories that are often based on state practice, but arbitrary limits on depositions and document production present more complex questions.

There have been suggestions that if judges would only use their authority to impose sanctions, all discovery problems could be solved. Promoting increased use of sanctions as a panacea for discovery problems is misleading. More judicial involvement in discovery will obviate the need for sanctions in many cases. It will also give the judge (or magistrate) sufficient familiarity with the case to discern more clearly when sanctions are appropriate. Although sanctions are not appropriate for directly curbing discovery activity, they should continue to be used to enforce judicial directives in aid of discovery management. The information developed in this study suggests that sanctions are not necessarily useful for overdiscovery problems. The reasons are related to the nature of the two general types of discovery abuse.

The Nature of Discovery Abuse

The line of demarcation between acceptable, proper use of the discovery process and abuse of that process is ill defined. Resistance to discovery is comparatively easy to identify and prevent when it takes the form of absolute refusal to produce relevant documents or to attend a deposition. Even then, there could be disagreement over whether the conduct constituted abuse of the process. Identifying overdiscovery abuse is even more difficult. Quite often, one person's abuse is another person's necessity. In short, it is more difficult to define and identify discovery abuse when the conduct involves overdiscovery. When abuse occurs, it is more expensive if it involves overdiscovery. It is more easily handled and usually less costly if it involves resistance. However, because abuse is so difficult to define, the term should be used carefully. The word "abuse" is almost inflammatory in some contexts, and its imprecision does not help advance the reasoned development of solutions. Instead of focusing on abuse, rule-makers and analysts should shift their attention to prevention and correction of discovery problems, recognizing that at some point a problem does cross the line and become abuse.

Professionalism and Ethics

Control of discovery and discovery costs in the American legal system should not have to depend only on rules and judicial control. Independent of this study, senior practitioners discussing discovery problems with federal district judges described discovery conduct they considered abusive, adding that they had engaged in such conduct themselves and that judges should not allow them to do so. On the one hand, the adversary system itself leads to some discovery problems, and attorneys might not fully represent their clients if they hold back: the judge can help by restraining them. On the other hand, restraint based on professionalism would seem to play a role in controlling discovery.

Judicial Awareness of Costs

Our interviews with both attorneys and judges indicated that in most cases, judges do not know how much discovery costs. Those who were actively involved early in the case had a better notion of the relative burden of discovery, but even with a discovery plan the real costs are not obvious because plans do not include estimates of discovery cost. Some method by which a judge could be informed about the estimated costs of discovery in a case would seem to be worth considering--not for purposes of controlling costs, but to help the judge assess discovery plans in a case that may result in extensive or disproportionate discovery.

Broader Implications

In one respect, problems of overdiscovery can be said to grow out of modern notice pleading. That view has been debated frequently before. It was discussed while the new rules were being formulated[19] and at the seminars held throughout the country to introduce the new rules,[20] and it has been discussed in other forums since that time.[21] The difference between today and the 1930s and 1940s may lie in the disproportionate growth of large-scale litigation and in the changed function of litigation in

---

19. See, e.g., 23 A.B.A.J. 965, 969 (1937).

20. Proceedings of Washington and New York Institutes on the Federal Rules of Civil Procedure (E. Hammond ed., A.B.A. 1938); Proceedings of Cleveland, Ohio Institute on the Federal Rules of Civil Procedure (A.B.A. 1938).

21. Claim or Cause of Action: A discussion on the need for amendment of Rule 8(a)(2) of the Federal Rules of Civil Procedure, 13 F.R.D. 253 (1952); Clark, Special Pleading in the "Big Case," 23 F.R.D. 45 (1957).

our society.[22] Changes in the substantive law, new rules on standing, new causes of action emanating from both courts and legislatures, the increasing use of class actions, and a general increase in our society's size and complexity have all contributed to the changed legal environment.

Our study of problem cases suggested that overdiscovery was associated with large complex cases. Data from other sources indicate that this type of litigation has experienced disproportionate growth in recent years. Other Center research has studied the judge time devoted to various substantive case types in the district caseload. The Administrative Office of the United States Courts maintains records on the frequency of filings for each case type. Combining these two information sources enables us to estimate the relative growth of more complex cases. From 1968 to 1977, case types requiring twice as much judge time as the average civil case exhibited a filing increase of 385 percent, while total civil filings increased by 83 percent.

During the past thirty years, there has been a blossoming of judicial techniques for managing complex litigation and a recognition on the part of both bench and bar that these cases require special attention by judges. This normally involves early intervention and continuous participation in the case. When this recognized need is viewed in the context of the change in the role of the courts and the growth in the quantity of complex cases, the chorus of complaints about discovery problems becomes more understandable.

Recommendations

Our recommendations are twofold. First, a long-term solution to the problems we have reported will require several years and much additional research and study. Potential long-term solutions that should be considered include establishing several procedural tracks for civil cases. Not all

---

22. See, e.g., Chayes, The Role of the Judge in Public Law Litigation, 89 Harv. L. Rev. 1281 (1976).

cases need extensive judicial intervention; many require very little. Over the next few years, our goals should include development of both better methods for handling cases with overdiscovery problems and simplified, less formal, less costly procedures for cases that do not require the full panoply of devices provided by the rules.

Second, the best short-term solution to the discovery problems we have discussed lies in judicial control. To facilitate the broader and more selective use of the best existing techniques, consideration should be given to revising the rule governing pretrial procedures.

We recommend establishing a rule to set forth a structure and suggested methods for case management from the time of filing to trial or other disposition. The most appropriate form for such a rule would be a major amendment to rule 16, perhaps including the provisions of proposed new rule 26(f) (see item 4 below). The title of the rule could be changed to "Pretrial Case Management" to more accurately reflect its scope. This amended, expanded rule should:

1. State that each case is unique, that a variety of management methods may be appropriate in individual cases, and that the judge should determine as soon as feasible the type and extent of pretrial case management procedures to be applied to each case

2. Emphasize the equal importance of identifying cases that do not warrant elaborate pretrial procedures and the attendant expense

3. Authorize the court, on its own initiative, to set limits on the time for and scope of discovery

4. Provide for an early conference to establish a schedule and plan for discovery, including determining the proper scope and direction of discovery and steps the attorneys plan to take to minimize total discovery costs

5. Provide that in appropriate cases, as part of the information upon which planning would be based, the judge should consider requiring each attorney to provide an initial estimate of discovery costs, not in order to monitor adherence to it, but to give the judge a sense of the size, nature, and probable costs of discovery

6. Note that the process of focusing and simplifying issues can start at the first conference, while recognizing that in some cases refinement of the issues cannot occur until the parties have conducted discovery

7. Require the court to consider the feasibility and desirability of assigning pretrial supervision to a magistrate

8. Provide for a settlement conference at the request of a party or at the discretion of the court

9. Provide for a final pretrial conference encompassing the provisions of present rule 16.

The amended rule would allow a flexible set of case management procedures to be applied according to the needs of each case. Although the rule's initial policy statement would emphasize the need for differentiated treatment--and the need to avoid rigid adherence to one set of procedures for every case--it would not set up a formal system for "tracking" cases through the rules of procedure.

This recommendation does not represent a major change from the approach used by many federal judges today. It does, however, require that each federal district judge consider what is needed to control discovery most effectively in each case. In so doing, it may increase the demands on already overburdened federal judges. Several other steps should be taken to address that problem by increasing the resources and capacity of the court system. These include:

1. Expansion of specialized training for judges in the substantive law of cases that have a large volume of discovery or are otherwise complex

2. Renewed consideration of whether these types of cases warrant special assignment

3. Increasing the use of magistrates to supervise discovery and providing specialized training for magistrates as recommended for judges in item 1 above

4. Development of short courses on discovery control for new judges and magistrates.

Our final recommendation for short-term improvement is to expand development of a set of case management guides. The <u>Manual for Complex Litigation</u> is an appropriate collection of suggested methods and techniques for managing complex cases; a separate guide or compendium should be prepared for non-complex cases. Its development should be closely coordinated with the Board of Editors of the <u>Manual</u>. Further, a system for continuing evaluation of the methods presented in each of these documents should be established, allowing periodic revision to incorporate the experience of judges and magistrates.

APPENDIX

CASE STUDIES

The six cases described in this appendix are among the twenty-three selected for study and analyzed in preceding parts of this report. These six cases, five of which are from the overdiscovery category, were singled out for detailed discussion to amplify our earlier observations about the discovery process and the effects on discovery of variables in each case. The names of the actual cases, participants in them, and some factual details have been changed to ensure confidentiality.

Profett College v. Area Accrediting Association

Profett College was managed as a close proprietary corporation. The corporation was owned by several members of one family. Although Profett College had been in existence for about fifty years, its unaccredited status led the brightest students to enroll for their first year of study but transfer elsewhere for the second year. The college had sought accreditation several times during the past decade, only to be rebuffed each time. Solely because the college was proprietary, the regional association of schools, colleges, and universities would not even consider granting academic accreditation. The college recruited a new president, who pursued accreditation more vigorously.

When it was clear that the association would once again resist an accreditation review of the college solely on the basis of its proprietary status, the college's owners retained counsel--first to reinforce their claims before the association, and then to consider litigation if accreditation was again refused.

The attorney, Eliot, had represented a member of the Profett family in a recent suit over a real estate transaction. Eliot was a forty-five-year-old partner in a three-person law firm. His was a general corporate practice in which he represented local businesses. He had no prior experience in the law pertaining to educational institutions, although he did have some experience in antitrust matters.

As a first step in the Profett College case, Eliot attempted, over the course of several months, to convince the association to consider accrediting the college. Eliot found that the president of the association firmly opposed even beginning the accreditation process, and although the association board did not unanimously support him, he was able to prevail. When the association refused to reconsider its accreditation policy, the Profetts brought suit under the federal antitrust laws, alleging an unreasonable restraint of trade and asking for an injunction against the association's enforcement of its no-proprietary-membership rule.

Counsel for the association was Lowell, who had represented the group for five years. Lowell's initial view was that the complaint was too broad. In his answer, he stated that the antitrust laws did not apply to educational institutions, and even if they did, the association had no intention of restraining trade, had no impact on relevant prices, and did not cause any exclusion of Profett College from relevant markets.

In an amended complaint, the Profetts added a second count, alleging the novel theory that the process of accrediting an educational institution is so inherently governmental in nature that the function is state action in a constitutional sense, and is therefore subject to the restraints of due process procedures.

The pleadings were completed in the first six months of the litigation, but protracted discovery extended the case over the next two-and-a-half years. Eliot estimated that about ten depositions were taken during this time. (The case file showed that thirty-two depositions were taken.) Both Eliot and Lowell agreed, in recalling the case, that discovery began with the exchange of two sets of interrogatories. Neither lawyer recalled the interrogatories as particularly long or onerous. (The case file showed that the plaintiff filed two sets of interrogatories with a total of thirty-three questions. The defendant served one set consisting of twenty-four questions.)

What, then, was the problem? Lowell thought that all discovery could have been conducted through interrogatories and requests for the production of documents. Indeed, as a general matter he favored confining discovery to these methods. Eliot, on the other hand, thought that in this type of litigation, depositions provided a good test for potential witnesses and theories that might be used at trial.[23]

No discovery was ever conducted on the second count of the complaint, although by the time of trial Eliot was prepared for argument with two witnesses. On the first (antitrust) count, Eliot thought his "best line of depositions" was of college registrars and admissions officers, concerning the weight they assigned to the accredited status of a college in reviewing the applications of its graduates or students seeking transfer to other colleges and universities.

These depositions were the only time that Eliot and Lowell saw each other face-to-face before the trial. Both Eliot and Lowell were busy with other trials during the course of the Profett litigation. Because Lowell had several out-of-town antitrust trials, Eliot felt that his opponent was unavailable "for months at a time." Most of the litigation documents were handled by a young associate of Lowell's. Lowell's office was somewhat larger than Eliot's and had greater experience in antitrust matters. In retrospect, Eliot thought that the different sizes of the two firms might have made the discovery more protracted than it otherwise would have been.

---

23. In this case, counsel seemed to disagree in fundamental ways about the function of discovery; yet the antitrust statutes, with their sweeping and vaguely worded provisions, would seem to encourage a great deal of discovery. See 2 National Commission for the Review of Antitrust Laws and Procedures, Report to the President and the Attorney General 33-45 (1979).

At the time suit was filed, the district had a master calendar and did not convert to an individual calendar system until the twenty-sixth month of the litigation. Eight months before the trial, the case was assigned to a single judge, although a defense motion for such assignment had been denied before the individual calendar was in operation. The assigned judge heard motions for summary judgment and ordered pretrial statements of the case. Judgment was rendered for the plaintiff.

Pease v. The Psychometric Institute

In the fall of 1975, Lane, an attorney, attended a meeting of the Physiopsychic Society, a group concerned with promoting good nutritional habits and educating the medical profession about the value of ortho-molecular and nutritional treatments in lieu of drugs. At the meeting, the president of the society introduced Lane to Pease, a young man who wanted to bring suit against the Psychometric Institute, a private psychiatric hospital in which he had been a patient for a five-year period that had ended nearly three years earlier. At Pease's request, and just before the three-year statute of limitations was tolled, Lane filed suit, even though 70 percent of his practice involved criminal defense work.

The complaint alleged that during Pease's initial medical check-up, which was a regular part of the hospital's admissions process, the examining doctor had misdiagnosed a chronic, organic condition as a mental disorder, and further, that five treating psychiatrists at the hospital had later done the same thing. Since all psychiatrists are medical doctors by training, this alleged misdiagnosis amounted to medical malpractice. Actual damages of $8 million and exemplary damages of $13 million were asked from all the defendants.

Timely answers were made by all the defendants, who were represented by five counsel: one for the hospital and its insurance carrier; one retained by the hospital later, in case judgment were to exceed the maximum liability coverage; one for two uninsured defendants; another for two psychiatrists who carried professional liability insurance; and another for the remaining defendant. Among the defense counsel were partners in a large, urban law firm (ninety-five attorneys); a partner in a local ten-person firm specializing in malpractice defense work; and a senior associate in a middle-sized law firm (forty-nine attorneys) in another city.

One of the defense counsel knew of Lane through reading the slip opinions of the state supreme court, which had rebuked Lane for inflammatory statements to juries in criminal cases.

Lead counsel for the defense was Danauer, the partner in the ten-person specialty firm whose main office was in the same county as the hospital. In the early stages of the defense, the hospital's counsel, Overholt, did nothing but monitor the action, although the hospital was concerned that any settlement or judgment would reflect badly on its business and reputation. The hospital's owner was adamantly opposed to any settlement.

Danauer's general discovery strategy was to assess the plaintiff's character and personality and to estimate how well or badly Pease could be portrayed before a jury. Although the first discovery events were three sets of interrogatories that the defense propounded to the plaintiff in the ninth through the thirteenth month of the litigation, the first deposition of the plaintiff was taken in the sixteenth month. All five counsel attended this deposition, which took a day and a half, but Danauer and Overholt conducted most of the questioning. They proved to have very different styles. Danauer asked few challenging questions, while Overholt constantly attempted to provoke Pease. However, he met with little success; both lawyers discovered that Pease had little interest in the proceedings, answering briefly and unemotionally. He seemed withdrawn rather than combative. Defense counsel left this opening deposition feeling that Pease would project his personality poorly before a jury.

The defense propounded a total of six sets of interrogatories to the plaintiff, but the plaintiff filed no interrogatories. Motions to compel answers were made and granted on behalf of several of the defendants. Most of the discovery was conducted by deposition; the defendants noticed twelve, and the plaintiff, five. Defense-initiated depositions were conducted with expert witnesses across the country, with the plaintiff's family, and with three family doctors.[24]

All the depositions were taken during three months immediately preceding trial. Lane complained that he was being deliberately kept away from his work preparing for other trials. When he raised these objections, the defense challenged him with a "let's find a judge" attitude that they knew he didn't have time for. The defense counsel insisted that the required establishment of a national standard of care for malpractice cases necessitated all of this travel; the defense also felt compelled to assess the impression that various experts would make on the jury.

The defense's "best witness," Danauer thought, was recruited by Overholt: he was a professor of medicine in a distant state university who did not appear stiff or overly professional. He was able to parry jokes with Lane, who had a folksy manner. The plaintiff's best witness (in Danauer's view) was a practicing psychiatrist who endorsed the nutritional theories of the plaintiff's complaint and had used some of them in treatment. The defense felt that this witness held his opinions firmly and would make a plausible, though perhaps too authoritarian, appearance before the jury. "We'd better get our wagons in a circle on this one," one defense lawyer said after hearing him.

The defense strategy was to press the three plaintiff's witnesses to test how far they were willing to go with their nutritional theories of the case, asking, for instance, "Doctor, do you mean that the white toast my wife served me this morning was poison?" Lane did little cross-examining

---

24. Litigation against psychiatrists is still in its formative stages. Furrow, <u>Defective Mental Treatment: A Proposal for the Application of Strict Liability to Psychiatric Services</u>, 58 B.U.L. Rev. 391 (1978). Further, the adoption of a national standard of care for these cases will encourage a great deal of travel for the deposition of expert witnesses. For a recent case, see Shilkret v. The Annapolis Emergency Hospital Association, 278 Md. 187, 349 A.2d 245 (1975), noted in <u>Survey of the Maryland Court of Appeals' Decisions 1975-76</u>, "Torts," 37 Md. L. Rev. 212 (1977).

during the defense-initiated depositions. He thought that to do so would give away much of his trial strategy, though he later admitted that this tactic perhaps depended too much on his background as a criminal defense attorney. He realized that much of the ortho-molecular and nutritional medicine that had allegedly worked to cure the plaintiff's condition after he had left the hospital was not widely accepted in the medical world. Those theories could not be presented directly, but would have to be introduced to challenge the medical and psychiatric judgment of the defense experts--to make them generalize (in the deposition) so as to exclude the plaintiff's theories and then (at the trial) invite their attention to the omission. In several depositions, Lane attempted to pursue orthodox medical thinking in order to make a psychiatrist admit that he was an M.D., qualified in medicine. With such admissions, Lane could then hope to impeach their credibility with their nonrecognition of various nutritional approaches.

One important deposition of a plaintiff's expert, taken about five months before the trial and one month before a routine, judicially imposed cutoff date, revealed that Pease was given a battery of psychological tests, one of which showed that he had serious mental problems. The expert seemed to the defense to be unprepared to explain these results.

By the end of the depositions, the plaintiff's claim was that his chronic physical condition was the result of nutritional deprivation. The defense claimed that there was no such thing as a chronic condition of the type from which the plaintiff allegedly suffered.

The trial, twenty-one months after filing of the suit, resulted in a verdict for the defendants.

Stuffing Pipe Associates v. Prime Construction, Inc.

The owner of a tract of land wanted to construct a commercial office building on the site. To that end, he entered into a contract with Prime Construction (PC), and PC entered into a subcontract three weeks later with Stuffing Pipe Associates (SP), an oral partnership. The subcontract was executed by Abel, for Abel and Warner, Inc. There was no such corporation, but Warner was indeed the partner of Abel in SP. Under the agreement between Stuffing Pipe and Prime Construction, SP was to provide all the plumbing, heating, air-conditioning, and ventilation infrastructure for the building.

The subcontract did not expressly require SP to provide blueprints of its work. It referred instead to completion of the work according to "drawings on file" with PC. Work proceeded smoothly in laying the ground floor. The "sleeves" (galvanized pipes necessary to provide future ducts for SP's infrastructure) were laid and the concrete flooring was poured around them. This process became more complicated with the second floor: PC's "sleeve" drawings were not in accord with the drawings presented by the steel fabricator-supplier for supporting beams. The owner, who retained the contractual power to review and approve all plans, disapproved the sleeve drawings on this account, and PC requested SP to supply it with plans that would not require the sleeves to cut through any steel.

SP protested, but within a week submitted drawings, which the owner disapproved as too vague. PC again requested "mechanicals" from SP, but a month of working time was lost to this delay. This sequence of events was repeated with each floor. Four months were lost on the third floor, six months more on the fourth and last floor. About half of this time was attributable to the owner's slowness in approving the redrafted sleeve drawings.

With minor exceptions, SP's work was completed two years and two months after its subcontract was signed. From the inception of the dispute over who would supply the sleeve drawings, PC had withheld half of the progress payments under its $500,000 subcontract with SP because the owner had withheld comparable amounts from PC. PC withheld the funds because it expected the owner to assert the liquidated damage clause in the contract. PC held a conference with all its subcontractors and the owner. All the subcontractors except SP agreed to support PC in its own demand for damages. SP, which thought PC's case against the owner was contractually weak, refused to wait for payment. It sued PC on its contract; for interfering with its work by failing to obtain the owner's approval in a timely fashion, or delay occasioned by doing the drawings that SP had no obligation to submit; and for having to defend claims against its material suppliers. SP claimed damages of $60,000 on its contractual claim, $225,000 on its interference and delay claims, and $25,000 on the suppliers' claims.

In its answer, PC disclaimed any interference with SP's work and any knowledge of the suppliers' claims. And as new matter, PC alleged that it was due $200,000 in back charges for correcting SP's defective work and $75,000 in damages because of SP's delays in providing sufficient personnel, redesigning sleeve drawings, and installing in accordance with specifications incorporated by reference into the subcontract.

The parties' initial legal position was typical of that in many construction contract disputes. One party (PC) maintained that the work was not performed on time, that the other party (SP) had abandoned the job site prematurely, and that the other party's work had proved defective; the other party (SP) argued that payment for work adequately performed was being "warehoused" and that it would make no corrections without being paid for past work. If the timing was wrong, SP argued, that wasn't its responsibility.

The attorneys who practiced in the city and specialized in construction contract disputes were located in about six law firms. All were familiar with the other firms' work and clients. Clients tended to drift between firms; as construction firms moved from job to job in different capacities, they might have to hire different firms to represent them in order that the attorneys might avoid conflicts of interest.

The plaintiff, SP, was represented by Bailey. He had been practicing law for eighteen years and was a partner in a firm with twenty-five attorneys specializing in construction and government contracts. Bailey and four of his partners had formerly worked in the office of Singer, the defense counsel. Singer, who had been practicing for twenty-eight years, was senior partner in a somewhat smaller firm with a similar legal specialty; he had previously represented SP in other cases. Singer's office was understaffed when the suit was filed; Bailey's office was unfamiliar with its client, SP. Abel, a partner in SP, had approached Bailey about representing him after meeting him socially.

Discovery began four months after the suit was filed and continued for fourteen months thereafter until the dispute was settled. Bailey saw his initial efforts in discovery as an attempt to compensate for his client's poor, almost nonexistent bookkeeping. The first discovery event was Bailey's request for the production of documents and a set of interrogatories asking thirty-four questions--half of which began, "Identify all documents . . ." Three months later, when Bailey had not received answers to the interrogatories and no documents were produced, he filed a motion to compel answers and document production.

A month after the motion to compel was filed, it was withdrawn without any judicial action. The motion was mooted by the provision of answers to interrogatories and partial production of documents. PC, through Singer's memorandum opposing the motion, stated that its job site manager had been ill and only within the week was available to answer the interrogatories. The answers, as they related to questions asking for identification of documents, were in part (1) a listing of SP's invoice and billing dates; (2) an offer to permit inspection of the written communications relating to "job progress" between the owner and PC, since such documents were "too copious to list"; (3) an objection to identifying all documents relating to the performance of SP's work as "too vague and indefinite"; (4) an objection to providing documents that were in the possession of the owner; and (5) a technical denial that "any contract existed with Abel and Warner, Inc."

Two months after the motion to compel was mooted, Bailey took the job site manager's deposition. This was the only deposition noticed and taken; Bailey believed that depositions are rarely needed in construction cases.

Another three months passed, and the first date set for trial came and went. In the meantime, Bailey was organizing the documents that had been provided. In the seventh month of discovery and six weeks before the second trial date, Singer gave Bailey a set of twenty-nine interrogatories that were intended to identify the portions of SP's work that SP considered "complete," "delayed" (and by whom?), the subject of a contractual breach, or the object of the claims of its suppliers. In particular, the interrogatories asked what work was performed before, during, and just after the submission of the revised sleeve drawings.

Accompanying these interrogatories was a motion to amend PC's answer with a counterclaim. Bailey was surprised that it did not come sooner and indicated that he had expected such a motion earlier. He naturally was opposed, and his response for SP was a motion for a protective order. The interrogatories and accompanying document requests and the motion to amend were, he said, a "dilatory tactic" aimed at postponing trial a second time; they would require that Bailey devote a substantial amount of time to his responses when he would otherwise be preparing for trial.

By this time, the Internal Revenue Service had subjected SP's assets to a lien for unpaid taxes, and Bailey had gained IRS approval to switch the basis of SP's legal fees from an hourly rate to a contingent fee. Bailey's tactic was to press for an early trial, which SP needed to recover its claims for itself, its creditors, and the IRS. Singer knew of the financial bind SP was in--he had received a notice of the IRS lien.

Singer argued that a lack of "timeliness" in his discovery was insufficient to meet the demonstration of "annoyance, harassment, oppression or undue burden" required under rule 26(c). In particular, Singer said, SP had not discussed the "relative hardships" involved if the motion were granted; he had in mind balancing the information "lost" to the defendant against the cost to the plaintiff in responding. At this point, Singer felt that SP's "remaining asset was this lawsuit," so he concurred with Bailey in thinking that PC's lost information was really balanced against SP's financial needs.

Just before the date set for trial, the trial judge mooted the motion after the parties argued it formally. The motion was denied and the trial was postponed for three months in order to give Bailey time to prepare responses.

No discovery cutoff date or pretrial order was ever entered. About a month before the second postponed trial date, the parties began settlement discussions, and the case was settled for $60,000. PC incurred about $15,000 in legal fees, and SP paid Bailey one-third of the settlement figure.

Gibbs v. Autoco, Inc.

Gibbs and Hammer were employees of Magna Motors. Hammer was a general mechanic in Magna's shop, and Gibbs had been with Magna for forty years, first as a mechanic and more recently as a service-ticket writer.

Hammer had in his service bay a vehicle registering 2,500 miles on its odometer. The owner complained of "hesitation when accelerating" and "rough idling." Hammer adjusted the idle and suggested that Gibbs accompany him on a test drive. Hammer backed the vehicle to the shop door. Then Gibbs took over the driving, drove to the edge of Magna's lot, stopped, and drove onto the abutting street, which sloped down to a curve in the roadway.

Going into the turn, Gibbs held the accelerator halfway down. Eyewitnesses reported that the car made a loud noise and then accelerated in the turn. Gibbs applied the brakes, but the car continued to accelerate, left the roadway, and went over the curb and down a slight embankment where it collided with a tree thirty feet from the street. Gibbs's face and neck were lacerated as he was thrown forward into the windshield frame and the steering column. Hammer received serious head injuries as he was also thrown into the windshield, which shattered around his head.

Nearby police pulled both Gibbs and Hammer from the wrecked automobile. Both were in the hospital, Gibbs for a week and Hammer for several months. Gibbs returned to work four months later, but Hammer was unable to return to his former job. Workers' compensation claims were filed and eventually paid by the World-Wide Guaranty and Insurance Company.

World-Wide took subrogation rights from Gibbs and Hammer. Just before the statute of limitations ran on Gibbs and Hammer's cause of action, World-Wide instructed Austen, an attorney, to file suit. Austen had represented World-Wide in many workers' compensation cases involving automobile dealerships across the state. He had practiced law in the state for twenty years.

One day before the statute of limitations was to toll the action, Austen filed suit against Autoco, the manufacturer of the vehicle. His complaint contained three theories: negligence in tort; express and implied warranty in contract; and strict liability, a theory up to then unrecognized in the state. Process was served on Autoco's attorney only after he had received in the mail the forty-two interrogatories that were filed with the complaint. The interrogatories had many subparts and contained about 150 separate questions.

Autoco's attorney, Baker, had practiced for three years with the largest firm (sixty attorneys) in the largest city in the state. He answered the complaint just after the forty-five days allotted. Regarding the first theory, Baker admitted a duty of care in the manufacture of automobiles and denied the rest; as to the second theory, Baker denied generally and specifically that Autoco's advertisements constituted any type of warranty; on the strict liability theory, the answer was silent. But with the answer, Baker moved to dismiss the third count under Federal Rule of Civil Procedure 12(d), arguing that the state had not adopted any rule of strict liability in this type of case.

Austen opposed Baker's motion with the argument that the state courts had not rejected the theory; indeed, several trial courts had refused to dismiss complaints based on strict liability. Austen requested an oral hearing on this matter. Both Austen and Baker had debated the question previously, before a group of negligence and malpractice attorneys who periodically assembled to discuss matters of importance to their legal specialties.

A week after he received the plaintiff's interrogatories, Baker responded with a set of sixty-eight interrogatories that contained more than 200 questions. On this first and only exchange of interrogatories, Baker inquired (inter alia) into the factual background of the complaint's allegation that the "accelerator mechanism, the carburetor, or the motor mounts" failed and thereby either caused or contributed to the accident. Austen answered that he was proceeding on a theory that the vehicle was generally defective and that he did not need to be more specific because further discovery and investigation would develop this point. Baker responded in kind: the answers to Austen's interrogatories were no more than "a holding action" (Baker's phrase), subject to supplementation later.

In the middle of the third month of litigation, a first conference was held with the federal judge. He inquired about the progress of discovery, and the description he was offered reflected an impasse. Both attorneys then suggested that the case be certified to the state supreme court for a decision on strict liability. (The jurisdiction's United States district courts, applying state law, had reached conflicting decisions on the issue.) The judge agreed, and a joint request for certification was filed within a month. The state court accepted the certification, and the federal court case was stayed for the next year while the state proceedings were held. This interval gave Austen time to investigate the reasons for the vehicle's failure.

The investigation proved difficult. Both Austen and Baker had run a title search of the vehicle. This had enabled Baker to trace its ownership, and he found that Autoco had purchased and stored the car after the accident. Austen traced the vehicle to a suburban body shop and suggested Baker meet him to examine it. Austen went to the car, and Baker, to the office of the last owner prior to Autoco. Finally the attorneys did get together, each accompanied by an expert, to inspect the mangled vehicle. The car had been partly stripped for parts, though the components alleged defective in the complaint were still present. The vehicle was photographed, but it was extremely dirty and Austen's expert mechanic had difficulty finding anything wrong. The mechanic wanted to perform some additional electrical tests; the parties agreed to meet again.

In the interval between meetings, the vehicle was moved again, to be stored outdoors in the winter cold. The second series of tests was conducted like the first--Austen's expert did the testing, and Baker's stood nearby, observing--and the tests were inconclusive. Austen's expert surmised that because no fault was found in the accelerator assembly, the carburetor must be at fault.

Just after what Austen described as this preliminary testing of the car, Baker gave notice that he wanted to depose Hammer, Hammer's wife, and Austen's two mechanical experts. The Hammers' depositions concerned mainly medical matters and the loss of income resulting from Hammer's injuries. Hammer had been given "shelter employment" at Magna's automobile parts desk (a job he held until two weeks after the court confirmed the jury verdict a little over a year later). However, Baker's notice of deposition to Austen's experts was opposed on the grounds that the experts were not yet "employed in anticipation of litigation." Austen stated that he did not intend to call either one as a witness at trial, and the judge stayed the depositions.

Austen was dissatisfied with the tests that had been performed on the car and the fact that no malfunction had been found. He felt uneasy about presenting the results to a jury, but he had little other evidence by the ninth month of the litigation (as it turned out, about a year away from the start of the trial). He then heard of a successful plaintiff in a state court case halfway across the country. The case involved a carburetor that Austen thought might be similar to the one in the Autoco vehicle. He called the plaintiff's attorney in that case and asked him to examine Austen's photographs of the vehicle for similarities. The attorney agreed, and Austen dispatched an associate to travel by airplane with the pictures.

The associate reported back that the carburetors in the two cases were not the same model, but that the consulting attorney had suggested that the associate show the photographs of the engine to a mechanic who had testified in several carburetor-related cases around the country. The mechanic, Vern, looked at the three photographs of the carburetor and observed that "the secondary throttle plates appeared to be not completely closed," which would account for the loud noise the police eyewitnesses heard at the scene of the accident. Austen employed Vern and paid his way to the garage where the vehicle was stored, only to find that the carburetor and its linkages had been removed. Austen stormed into Baker's office, but Baker was totally unaware of the removal.

The carburetor assembly was never located, but Vern informed Austen that a technical service bulletin issued by Autoco years earlier had referred to sticking plates, the same problem he observed in the photographs. Magna Motors told Austen that the only copy it had of the bulletin was, the service manager's personal copy; Austen obtained a photocopy of the bulletin from sources several counties away. The bulletin did indeed refer to the plate opening as if it were a widespread or general problem. Austen's experts, including Vern, tinkered with a friend's car, hoping to duplicate what Gibbs and Hammer said had happened to the vehicle in the accident, but they were unable to do so.

Meanwhile, in the fifteenth month of litigation, the state supreme court, in deciding the question certified to it by the federal court, embraced the theory of strict liability for its jurisdiction, the judge set discovery cutoff and trial dates, and the federal court case was reactivated with three sets of depositions. The transcript of each set was about seventy-five pages long. The first set involved Gibbs and Hammer. Gibbs proved a poor witness, surprising his attorney with his knowledge of state-of-the-art automobile mechanics (his working experience with autos had ended thirty years earlier) and body language that contradicted what he said. From Austen's point of view, Hammer fared little better. Baker's line of questioning on whether the car's radio was on and whether Gibbs or

Hammer was smoking at the time of the accident led nowhere. Baker had hoped to establish a connection with Gibbs's medical history of kidney disability and respiratory infections, for which he took daily medication. In deposition, the owner of the vehicle stated that he had taken it into Magna Motors for a tune-up and what Gibbs, who wrote the service ticket, described as "hesitation"—one short pause before the accelerator assembly responded to pedal pressure. Finally, six weeks before trial, Baker took the depositions of three police eyewitnesses. Their station house was 100 yards from the accident site. They reported having heard a loud noise from the vehicle and seeing its front end lift up as it accelerated while the brakes locked.

These depositions produced several disputes over the relevance of questions but no motions for sanctions. There were no requests for documents: everything was either voluntarily provided (in the case of some police photographs, for which the police had lost the negatives, the two sides shared the pictures) or stipulated to. Austen often preferred to obtain documents through his contacts in other dealerships rather than "tip off" Autoco to what he was doing. The argument over whether to depose Austen's two experts (not Vern, who was the third) was resolved in a compromise arranged in the judge's chambers: the first one Austen consulted, who found nothing, was issued a protective order; the second was deposed five weeks before the trial.

Four weeks before the trial, at the pretrial conference, Austen still asserted his "general defect" theory, but announced that Vern would testify at the trial about the secondary throttle plates. Within ten days of this conference, Vern had examined the car, but he never was deposed because the cutoff date had passed. Autoco provided Baker with an expert who had testified about carburetor problems many times over the past eight years. Austen, who was familiar with the expert's testimony in past cases, did not depose him, but conceded later that he did not do so because of a tacit understanding with Baker to permit Vern to testify without a prior deposition. The six-day trial was thus a battle of experts before the jury, who returned a $30,000 verdict for Gibbs and $650,000 for Hammer.

Smith v. Ajax, Inc.

On a misty, slushy evening, Smith was driving a rented car on a limited-access highway undergoing reconstruction, within the boundaries of a large city. Smith and his companion were both wearing seat belts across their laps; the passenger also wore a shoulder restraint. While proceeding at about forty miles an hour through the construction area, Smith's mid-sized American car collided head-on with another vehicle, driven by Jones. At the time, Jones was driving the wrong way in the slow, right-hand lane provided for oncoming traffic. He had just entered the roadway, but had been misled by, misunderstood, or failed to heed directional signs designed to assist motorists through the construction site. Jones's truck was owned by his employer, for whom Jones was working when the collision occurred. Jones was severely injured, Smith's passenger received minor abrasions and a fracture, and Smith was killed instantly when the collision pitched him forward into the steering column, dashboard, and windshield. Evidence at this time showed that Smith's shoulder restraint was cut out, either by rescue workers at the scene of the accident, or earlier by the rent-a-car company.

Smith was a professional man in his thirties; he had a steady job and was expecting a promotion. He was separated, but not divorced, from his wife. His wife's attorney, Lewis, eleven months after the accident, brought a wrongful-death/survival action for negligence against Jones and his employer; against the rent-a-car company and Ajax, its parent corporation, for the express and implied violation of the rental contract for the car and violation of federal and state safety regulations in failing to provide a car with a collapsible steering assembly and shoulder restraints, and for failing to maintain and inspect the car; against the highway construction company for negligence in misdirecting Jones; and against the state highway department for negligent supervision of the construction site. These actions were consolidated for a jury trial as demanded by the plaintiff. The local franchise holder of the rent-a-car company was bankrupt and was therefore not sued.

Besides Lewis, there were six counsel of record: Crow for the automobile manufacturer; Green for the rent-a-car company, its franchisee, Ajax, and their insurer; Wilson for Jones and his employer; one for the seat belt component manufacturer and its corporate parent; another for the highway construction company; and another for the state.

These attorneys were hired in different ways. Lewis's firm had a policy of taking cases in which, he said, "hopeless maiming or injury" was involved. In such cases he worked on a contingent-fee basis. However, his firm did not usually accept personal injury work because such cases often involved work for major insurance companies, whose restrictions on expenditures and fees the firm found onerous. Crow was a member of a three-person law firm that had successfully represented the auto manufacturer in a previous case. The manufacturer either reserved the right to retain counsel in its insurance policies or was self-insured, depending on the claim. It retained Crow directly. On the other hand, Green was retained by the insurer of the rent-a-car company under an insurance policy that did not give Ajax the same control over the selection of counsel. Green was a partner in a three-person suburban law office. Wilson was hired by Jones's employer's insurance company. Only Lewis had access to the library and personnel resources of a large firm.

"I never had a case I knew less about at the start," Lewis said. With the complaint, he also filed a request for production of documents from the rent-a-car company. He requested acquisition, testing, and maintenance documents for the car involved in the accident; the car's entire rental history, along with any customer complaints about it as well as the general complaint file of the rent-a-car company; all the company's employees' names and addresses; the accident reports, studies, and investigatory files; the records of Smith's rental; the incorporation papers, bylaws, and annual reports of the rent-a-car company and Ajax; safety regulation compliance records; the rent-a-car company's franchisee's manuals for car maintenance, operation, and the hiring and training of the franchisee personnel, as well as business policy papers of the franchisee and its parent firm insofar as they pertained to the franchisee; and all other "relevant" documents.

One day before the end of the thirty days allowed for answering the request under the federal rules of civil procedure, Green filed his responses. He agreed to gather the requested documents, with the following exceptions: (1) accident reports prepared "in anticipation of this litigation"; (2) the incorporation papers, bylaws, and annual reports of the rent-a-car company and Ajax, which he deemed "irrelevant" to the litigation; (3) general complaint files and agency manuals for employee training, inspection, and maintenance of vehicles, and "policy papers," which he claimed were "too broad and burdensome"; and (4) the request for all other relevant documents, which he objected to as "too broad and vague."

A month after the responses were received, Lewis was given the acquisition, testing, and alteration documents for the car, its rental history, and the company employee lists. He then initiated a flurry of discovery events. He deposed the passenger and asked the representative of the automobile manufacturer to provide test data on the car's capabilities. He asked about the possibility of starting a car without first engaging the seat belt assembly, and about the operation of the buzzer and ignition systems. (At this point the first status-call conference was held.) Subsequently, Lewis filed the first of four sets of interrogatories with the manufacturer.

Moving in many directions simultaneously posed a dilemma for Lewis; having sued so many defendants, he feared "a loss of focus" if he made a detailed presentation of his case against all of them to the jury. Presentation of the case against the highway construction company and the state would diminish the impact he might otherwise expect against Jones and the companies responsible for the car. In successive interrogatories in response to his discovery attempts, moreover, Crow (the car manufacturer's attorney) was insisting on increased specificity about the particular part of the steering mechanism and seat belt assembly involved in any alleged malfunction.

In the fifth month after filing the complaint, Lewis supplemented his interrogatory answers to the manufacturer by noting that the transportation safety board had issued a report on the accident and found that although Smith's passenger had been wearing both a lap seat belt and shoulder harness, Smith had not been wearing a shoulder harness at the time of the accident. This was the first time Lewis knew this; before this point, the possibility existed that both restraints had been cut by the rescue workers. Whether a driver's shoulder harness existed in the car was never revealed. The report intensified Lewis's discovery problem because the manufacturer then insisted that, if no restraint existed, data on its construction and testing were not discoverable. After the fourth set of interrogatories was propounded to the manufacturer, Lewis sought and obtained a magistrate's order requiring the manufacturer to produce data on both the steering column and the seat belts. A month later, an automotive expert for the plaintiff examined the car, which was by then purchased and stored under the authority of the manufacturer. He could find nothing wrong with the steering mechanism.

The attorneys for the seat belt component manufacturer and its parent company also recognized the plaintiff's dilemma. When their expert was given notice of a deposition by Lewis, they attempted to condition his appearance on the dismissal of the liability claim against their clients. In reply, Lewis said that he now believed no shoulder restraint had been present but did not know this to be true. The seat belt attorneys filed for a protective order, which the magistrate denied; they appealed this ruling to the judge, who affirmed the denial.

Both Crow and the seat belt attorneys thus attempted to "play off" Lewis's lack of data on liability against his need for information on the utility of the seat belt in preventing injury. Lewis considered the attempt to condition the appearance of a witness at a deposition "outrageous," particularly since the conditions were sought by entities still defendants in the lawsuit.

By the end of the fifth month, neither Lewis nor Green had received any further documentation from Ajax, the rent-a-car company, or its franchisee, even though Green represented those parties. Lewis's inquiries were routed through Green, who then sent them to the insurer's regional office, where Green's contact was the senior claims examiner. The examiner routed them either to his home office or to the offices of the by-then former franchisee of the rent-a-car company. In some instances, the routing went to the home office of the insured, Ajax. All the document searches were undertaken by insurance company adjustors at the franchisee's warehouse, and when they were unsuccessful, Green was informed that the requested records and documents must be at another location--a second warehouse 150 miles from Lewis's office. Lewis proposed that they visit the second warehouse together and undertake a joint search. Green was unable to do so, and Lewis asked him to have someone from among the defendants he represented meet Lewis there. Green agreed. Lewis went on the appointed day and was not met. He found the warehouse deserted, and returned empty-handed and "furious."

The measure of Lewis's fury was the filing of a motion for a default judgment and an order compelling discovery of the internal operating procedures manuals from the rent-a-car company. He hoped to find "the smoking gun"--statements to the effect that franchisees should "save money and cut out the seat belts if they gave trouble." Finding statements about cutting costs would be second best. In support of both motions, Lewis recounted a four-month effort to secure the manuals and his unsuccessful trip to the distant warehouse: he argued that at the very least, Green was not taking control of the discovery effort; the only affidavits of searches were those of insurance company adjustors. In reply, Green argued that the documents existed, probably at three locations in two states, and he presented affidavits of search by a senior examiner of the insurance company at one of those locations. Green maintained that Lewis should have gone to the insurer's office in the area of the warehouse in order to gain access to it, and he recounted his "repeated efforts to gain compliance with [Lewis's] requests." The magistrate denied Lewis's default motion, but issued an order to produce the manuals in three weeks' time--in the eighth month of the litigation.

Discovery over the next three months involved videotape and stenographic depositions of six employees of the auto manufacturer and seat belt component manufacturer. The attorneys for these defendants sought continuances and protective orders pending further discovery, contending that they should not be "discovered" first. Lewis sought to extend the time for executing an offer of judgment made by the seat belt company and its corporate parent pending further discovery, finally agreeing to a date five days after the deposition of one of the parent company's executives. Several requests for extensions of time in which to answer the four sets of interrogatories propounded by Lewis to the auto manufacturer were also made, granted, and resolved during this time. Finally, the manufacturer gave Lewis a first set of interrogatories consisting of forty-three questions on Smith's background, employment, medical history, and injuries.

In the middle of this three-month period, Green's deposition was taken. He reported success in assembling documents responsive to three of Lewis's twenty-five requests, and a failure to locate responsive documents for eleven requests, including those asking for the operating manuals. He said that the insurer had not searched any additional document centers. Finally, he described a conversation with a retired executive of the rent-a-car company, in which the executive said the record sought did not exist. To his deposition, Green brought documents responsive to five of Lewis's additional requests.

Shortly after this, Lewis made a second set of requests for the production of documents, inquiring into the relationship between the rent-a-car company, its franchisees, and Ajax. He suspected poor intercorporate relations. He also scheduled depositions on the check-out and check-in procedures for rental cars and asked the same defendants twenty-eight questions in a second set of interrogatories to them. He further deposed the seven automobile dealerships that had serviced the franchisee's rental cars. Finally, he attempted to depose the executive whom Green had identified as saying that the manuals did not exist.

At the end of all this activity, Lewis filed a motion for a default judgment for failure to comply with discovery. He cited nine apparently inconsistent statements Green made about the manuals and argued that the default sanction imposed in National Hockey League v. Metropolitan Hockey Club, 427 U.S. 639 (1976), was appropriate. In reply, Green apologized for any "misleading statements" he had made in the past, and said the requested manuals now appeared to be in the control of the franchise holder, who refused to produce them because he was involved in litigation with Ajax over other matters. Green demanded an oral hearing on the default motion. In response, Lewis stated that this was the first he had heard of Green's difficulties with the franchisee or even of its control over the manuals, "once said not to exist and now to exist in another's control." Lewis cited the nine positions Green had taken on the manuals over the course of discovery. At the oral hearing, Green argued his own case and described his repeated phone calls attempting to gain the cooperation of the insurer and the franchisee. In the thirteenth month of the litigation, the magistrate denied Lewis's default motion, citing Societe Internationale v. Rogers, 357 U.S. 197 (1958), and preferring its language over that of Metropolitan Hockey.

Jones and his employer were glad enough to witness Lewis's arguments with Ajax, its subsidiary, and its insurer--all of which deflected Lewis's attention from Jones. Both of these defendants were represented by Wilson, who had been retained by the insurance carrier holding the automobile policies for both Jones and Jones's corporate employer.

Although Wilson thought Lewis was pursuing Ajax as "the deepest pocket" in the case, he reported later that "the picture looked bleak" for his clients when the case first entered his office. Using his normal procedures for personal injury work, he sent a photographer to the collision site. Wilson found the pictures heartening. They showed a gap in the detour barriers between oncoming lanes just past the point where Jones had driven to the left to begin the detour and had continued driving left into the face of oncoming traffic. Jones had apparently driven through the gap and crashed shortly thereafter while he was attempting to regain the right side of the roadway (he told Wilson). Because the gap in the barriers showed up clearly in the photographs of the roadway, Wilson reasoned, it might be possible to negate the so-called boulevard rule, which presumed negligence when an automobile was driven the wrong way on a limited-access roadway. If there were no barriers, there was no limited access, and the rule might not apply in the area of the detour.

Wilson thought the barrier gap might also suggest negligence on the part of the highway construction company and the state. He researched the applicable traffic safety code for provisions affecting such questions. He also employed two experts on the design of detours, who told him about a detour procedures-and-design book uniformly used by construction companies to set up detours. This book clearly showed the need for barriers at the point where Jones crossed into oncoming traffic. One wave of interrogatories was exchanged between Wilson and the attorney for the construction company. After this exchange, the company deposed Wilson's two experts, but Wilson was satisfied that they stood up well under examination. Wilson also found that the state owned a warehouse full of detour barriers and that construction companies normally borrowed or rented barriers from this warehouse. Wilson deposed two officials of the state department of transportation to confirm that the state had procedures for checking the placement of these barriers at construction sites.

In all, Wilson felt that he was on his way to a sharing of the liability that he initially thought his clients would have to bear alone. So far, he had been representing both Jones and Jones's employer. The proof that he was working up suggested, however, that Jones might be successful in a cross-complaint against the highway construction company. Wilson was concerned about a conflict of interest if such a suit were filed, although the insurance carrier had urged the dual representation and Jones did not object when asked. Jones did then file a cross-complaint against the highway construction company. Following the filing, Wilson deposed the construction company's experts; he and Lewis questioned them about the use of the detour design book at the site. Part of Lewis's case was being built on the foundation of Wilson's work.

Lewis continued to pursue Ajax. The second status-call conference was held. In the eleventh month of the litigation, Lewis first deposed Green's source who said the manuals did not exist. This deposition was continued twice and was held off and on throughout the next nine months. It was renewed just before trial a year later. Once deposed, Green's source said that the records were in a distant, previously identified but unsearched storage center. He also reported that he had maintained chronological files while he worked for the rent-a-car company and that those files included letters saying "not to fool around with seat belts," policy letters to regional managers, and a complaint file.

This information was gleaned during the second year of discovery. At about the same time, Lewis was also deposing two members of Ajax's law department; both reported becoming aware of Lewis's interrogatories and first set of document requests only in the ninth month of the litigation. Once they were aware of the case, products liability specialists in Ajax's law department began to participate in the weekly review conference between the department and Green. Ajax's general counsel then had the rent-a-car company's case file transferred to the insurer's home office. Green's handling of the case was under constant review; Green himself soon concluded that he should resign his position as counsel to Ajax and the insurer.

By the twenty-third month, Lewis had deposed Ajax, its subsidiary, the insurance carrier, and Green, and was in a position to know the change of command he faced. That knowledge, coupled with the results of a deposition of a paralegal in Ajax's law department, made him renew his default motion. In the renewed motion he charged that "massive document destruction" had taken place during the litigation's eighth month. Lewis's basis for this charge was that the paralegal had stated in her deposition that the rent-a-car company had destroyed a "massive number of documents" at the record center far distant from Lewis's office. When she was dispatched to locate the manuals and files described by Green's source, she was told that the documents were destroyed as a part of Ajax's sale of a rent-a-car company, while Smith's wrongful-death action was pending.

Ajax's general counsel retained Diamond, a middle-level partner in a firm with resources equivalent to Lewis's. Green retained Crow (the attorney for the automobile manufacturer) as his personal counsel after the insurance carrier agreed to pay Crow's fee; Green struck his name from the record.

In support of his second default motion, Lewis recounted the nine representations Green had made to him about the long-sought operating manuals and argued that at some point Green should have known that many of those representations were false. Diamond answered that Lewis's discovery requests had not been circulated to Ajax until the eighth or ninth month of the litigation; that the former owner of the rent-a-car company had ordered the document destruction; and that the very fact that about ten replies were made concerning the existence and location of the manuals showed that a continuous search was being made and that no masterminded cover-up was intended. Indeed, Diamond argued, the various responses tended to show that Green was in continuous contact with the defendants and did not mastermind any deceit; no malice was shown in any event. Diamond maintained that no question of fact had ever been in dispute--that the driver's shoulder harness had been cut and removed long before the accident. On Green's behalf, Crow now argued that Green had passed along the results of the insurance company's efforts as they were reported to him; that Green had been in continuous contact with both the insurance company and, after the eighth month of the investigation, with Ajax itself; and that Green had been unable to convince the insurance company of the importance of the case until counsel from the insured's home office became actively involved in it.

The renewed default motion was denied by the magistrate and appealed to the judge, who upheld the denial. The plaintiff was awarded $55,000 in attorneys' fees, however, and after two more status calls, the judge cut off discovery at the end of the twenty-fifth month of the litigation.

In the twenty-fourth and twenty-fifth months of the litigation, discovery against the highway construction company was completed by interrogatory. One final problem remained: Just after the cutoff date, Lewis wanted to show the jury a two-minute film on the effect of not wearing seat belts. The film had been produced by an automobile manufacturer not involved in this litigation. Lewis sought and was granted a court order permitting deposition of the filmmakers to establish the film's authenticity. Three months later, the defendants filed a motion to take the deposition of an expert on the seat belt mechanism. Over Lewis's objection, the motion was granted, with leave to take the deposition at a time that would not interfere with the conduct of the trial.

The trial occurred thirty-eight months after the complaint was filed. Discovery had included seventeen depositions, ten sets of interrogatories, and four requests for document production. Lewis relied heavily on Wilson's experts and the detour design manual to "decimate" (Wilson's word) the construction company expert. He portrayed Ajax as careless in its attitude toward consumers; Diamond rebutted that picture by depicting Ajax as attempting to improve the consumer attitudes of a wayward subsidiary. The jury returned a $700,000 verdict for the plaintiff against Jones, his employer, and the highway construction company. Wilson reported that the courtroom was "in shock" when the verdict was announced. No verdict or judgment of liability against Ajax or its subsidiary was ever made; they paid nothing but part of Lewis's discovery cost. Jones recovered $90,000 on his cross-complaint.

Gastex, Inc. v. Amonil, Inc.

Gastex, a natural gas utility, was informed by its suppliers that they could not deliver gas so as to satisfy the increased demands Gastex had made on the pipeline companies during the past two decades. As part of a two-year search for alternative sources of gas, in mid-1973 Gastex executed an agreement with Amonil, a major oil company, to purchase a by-product of the crude oil refining process. The agreement was reached after ten months of negotiations between Amonil and Gastex executives and their attorneys.

The agreement was for Amonil to sell Gastex 5,500 barrels a day of an oil refinery by-product. The sale was to occur over a period of ten years, 1975 to 1985, at 12.5 cents per gallon, F.O.B. seller's refinery, subject to adjustment "by a barrel charge in the posted price of crude petroleum as reported in Blatt's Oilgram." At the end of the first five years of the contract, either party could request that the price be re-negotiated. The first delivery was to be no earlier than January 1, 1975 and no later than April 1, 1975, with the provision that Amonil could cancel the agreement if Gastex could not accept the first delivery by December 1, 1975. The specific price computation, to be made using Blatt's Oilgram prices, was provided in an attachment to the agreement and incorporated by reference: the price was to be computed using Blatt's posted prices for two production companies in the Southwest. The contract provided for liquidated damages at the rate of 1 cent per due and undelivered gallon.

The agreement's opening statements of contractual purpose witnessed Amonil's ample supplies of the by-product, which it agreed to load for shipment to Gastex. Amonil was to adapt the port facilities adjacent to its refinery for receiving the barges that would transport the by-product to Gastex. The contract also referred to the following actions on Gastex's part: First, two months before the agreement was executed, Gastex exercised an option to buy a fifty-acre site for a conversion plant to manufacture gas from the by-product. Second, a month before executing the agreement, Gastex had received a report from its economic consultants about the probable amount of synthetic gas its distribution system could handle. Gastex served 3 million people in three states; most of its customers had no other energy supply for heating, air-conditioning, or cooking. The economic consultants estimated that "firm future demand" for Gastex services would increase to 3.9 million customers by 1985. With that projection in hand, Gastex drafted a "definition of plant" and issued it to three general contractors, who were invited to submit bids for construction of the conversion plant. Within three months after the agreement was signed, two of the contractors had backed out, declining to submit the type of fixed-price bid Gastex sought.

The oil embargo of 1973 increased the demand for crude oil and decreased the supply. The mid-continent prices posted in Blatt's Oilgram were no longer the highest market prices, and the United States government froze the price of existing domestic crude oil in late 1973, with mandatory price controls. Despite the fact that new sources of oil were exempt from these controls, the freeze still presented a problem for Gastex and Amonil: how to compute the price escalation clause of the agreement. Because it was to be computed on the crude oil prices of two mid-continent production companies, the question arose whether new or exempt oil prices could form the basis for the computation, or some part of it (and what part?). Blatt's continued to report a stable and frozen price for old oil, but that did not reflect the embargo-inflated prices Amonil was paying for foreign crude oil delivered to the refinery from which Gastex's by-product was to be shipped. It was not until early 1976 that Blatt's started to report prices for new or unreleased crude oil.

Gastex negotiated for nine months with the one remaining general contractor willing to bid on a contract to construct its conversion plant. Those discussions came to naught, however, and Gastex then began to explore a joint venture with another gas utility whose service area was adjacent to its own. The adjacent utility had a conversion plant under construction, but was delaying its completion for fiscal reasons. It was willing to allow Gastex to participate as a joint venturer in its half-completed plant if Gastex would finance its share, which was calculated at about $20 million.

Throughout 1974, Amonil attempted to change the price definition in the contract. In September, it presented Gastex with new computations, 40 percent of which were based on the price of foreign crude oil. Gastex refused to accept Amonil's new computation, which would have increased the price from 17 cents to 26 cents per gallon. Gastex thereafter considered Amonil to be in default on the agreement. Amonil thought Gastex was refusing a reasonable method for computing the contract price after the imposition of price controls.

Gastex's in-house counsel retained a firm of forty partners and twenty associates, and in February, 1975, Gastex filed suit against Amonil for breach of the agreement. With the complaint, the plaintiff filed a first set of document requests and interrogatories. There were twelve interrogatories in all, each asking for the names and addresses of persons with knowledge of negotiations for the agreement. The document requests required Amonil to produce all drafts of the agreement, as well as all related correspondence and memoranda; its price schedule for refinery by-products; its correspondence and memoranda of meetings with federal energy agencies; and, finally, the records of all preparations for adapting the dockage facilities at its refinery to deliver the by-product to Gastex.

Amonil's attorneys, a law firm of forty partners and fifty-five associates, filed a timely response to the first interrogatories, providing the appropriate names of corporate officials. Amonil stated that its board of directors had never discussed the agreement and its executives had not kept abreast of Gastex's plans to build a gas conversion plant, except through the newspapers.

The contacts with federal agencies were only generally described as phone calls or meetings with the "general counsel's office" or "executive secretariats." In response to Gastex's other document requests, Amonil gave several answers: (1) much of the correspondence should already be in the plaintiff's hands; (2) surrendering the records of Amonil's in-house counsel would violate the attorney-client privilege; and (3) the request for many of the drafts of the agreement was harassment of Amonil. The defendant also reported that the lawyers had found no Amonil price schedule or records of sales of refinery by-products, no memoranda about details of meetings with federal agencies, and no records of adaptations at Amonil's refinery for delivering the by-product to Gastex.

At the same time that Amonil replied to Gastex's first interrogatories and document requests, it submitted its first interrogatories to Gastex. Ten interrogatories asked for the names and addresses of Gastex executives who contacted federal agencies, the adjacent gas utility, investment bankers, economic consultants, and Amonil during the ten months of contract negotiations. Amonil also asked for the names of officials responsible for Gastex's planning and budgeting for the proposed conversion plant and for its business in general. Gastex did not object to any of these questions and answered all of them. Amonil's first six requests for document production involved Gastex's 1972 to 1974 annual reports, consolidated balance sheets, budgets, budgetary changes, and documents on the sources of Gastex's funds. Gastex provided statements of actual capital expenditures, but declared that there were no documents related to potential fund sources.

This first wave of discovery was completed five months after the complaint was filed. Depositions of Amonil sales and marketing executives who had knowledge of the agreement began in the third month of the litigation.

In the sixth month of the litigation, the plaintiff had deposed two Amonil officials and initiated another set of interrogatories. Twenty-six questions were asked. They dealt with (1) the timing, plans, and expenditures for adapting Amonil's dockage facilities; (2) the prospective by-product sales (if any) that Amonil did not pursue because of its preparations to honor its obligations to Gastex; (3) the accounting procedures used to compute the per-gallon price of the by-product; (4) the terms of another Amonil contract to supply the by-product to another gas utility, in particular whether the defendant had recently sought to modify the price term governing that contract and whether the recently imposed federal allocation plan had affected that contract (and if so, how?); and (5) the origin and past use of the formula Amonil proposed to recompute the Gastex-Amonil price term.

Several of these inquiries reflected Gastex's problem in obtaining satisfactory assurances of future compliance from Amonil. After the federal allocation law went into effect, Amonil had to certify that it was willing to supply the by-product to Gastex. Amonil would provide this certification only if Gastex were a "baseline customer" (it was not). The federal government, in turn, would not even process the forms to allow Gastex to become a baseline customer without the Amonil certification. From Amonil's point of view, any certification of baseline supply would jeopardize its own supply lines to its petrochemical subsidiaries. Thus Gastex was interested in how other Amonil customers were being treated and the number of federal allocation forms Amonil received, processed, executed, and denied. Amonil's answers indicated it had not made any other by-product sales and had executed very few forms, the latter against the advice of in-house counsel.

Gastex followed these interrogatories with more document requests. Amonil filed its replies, after two informal extensions were granted, at the end of the eighth month of litigation and just after the first status-call conference with the judge, who ordered the parties to "continue discovery and report back in six months." In reply, Amonil said that it had not found, but was still searching for, federal energy allocation forms for specific other customers of Amonil; documents relating to the dock or refinery changes in abeyance because of Gastex's inability to take delivery; and "policy or position" papers on Amonil's certification of its customers' federal allocation forms. Just after the status call, Gastex deposed a dozen Amonil employees. In forty notices, Amonil deposed about eighty persons over the next six months.

Amonil's law firm had by then assigned about ten partners and an equal number of associates to work on several phases of the litigation. (Gastex's attorneys thought that about thirty had been assigned to the case.) The background of the partner who was billing Amonil was reflected in the law firm's approach to discovery. The partner's recent experience was variously perceived as construction contracts work and as "an accounting background" by one of his subordinates and an opposing counsel, respectively. Each of the firm's initial two lines of discovery reflected one of these perceptions. The first approach was to depose officials of the adjacent utility with which Gastex had proposed a joint venture. The objective of those ten to twenty depositions was to establish a timetable for the construction of the conversion plant. Amonil's attorneys wanted to be able to show that the construction timetable for such a plant would have made it impossible for Gastex to accept the first delivery within the time allotted by the contract. They pursued this line of questioning with the hope of establishing the adjacent utility's timetable for building its plant as well as hypothesizing a reasonable timetable for Gastex's own projected conversion plant. To lay a foundation for this line of questions, Amonil's attorney asked whether, as of the date of the agreement, the adjacent utility intended to carry through on the joint venture. The answer was "yes." Asking the same question as of a date several months later would have elicited a negative answer. Gastex's counsel were afraid of that question because of its impact on their client's ability to take delivery, but the question was never asked--in part because, even if Amonil's attorneys had realized that the joint venture had been dropped (the utility's suppliers had curtailed supplies, and the conversion plant's output was needed to satisfy local needs), they would still have wanted to pursue the issue of construction timetables.

The second line of Amonil's depositions was related to the first; it concerned Gastex's ability to finance its own plant or to participate in the joint venture. "Utilities are debt oriented," Gastex's attorneys later explained, "and debit accounts are the easy way to make out the need for a rate increase." Amonil reportedly knew this, because its officials, in attempting to renegotiate the price term, had suggested that the higher costs could be passed along to Gastex customers. However, the lead partner in Amonil's law firm examined Gastex's accounts and regarded its credit-worthiness as weak. Consequently, he took more than twenty depositions of investment bankers, large commercial banks, and underwriters of capital stock issues to determine Gastex's financial prospects in the capital marketplace. From the perspective of Gastex's attorneys, these depositions merely paralleled Gastex's own preliminary research on various funding devices, such as capital stock and bonds, which Gastex had considered at various times. Amonil's attorneys considered Gastex's financial planning weak and, more to the point, optimistic; the depositions of Gastex's banking community were intended to show that capital wasn't available to finance the construction even if the plant could have been produced on time. Gastex attorneys reported not being bothered by such lines of inquiry, and they paid little attention to the depositions.

Gastex attorneys halted these two lines of depositions several times for appearances before the judge. The question the plaintiff posed was, what are the issues and how do these depositions help to define them (and how many more depositions can we expect)? Only once did the judge intervene--and that was later, to prevent simultaneous depositions of Gastex employees.

Gastex's attorneys continued to believe that the case "could be won in a hundred-yard dash." The question at issue remained simple: was there a breach of contract by Amonil? This question revolved around the meetings and letters exchanged in September and October, 1974. Amonil's attorneys thought that the Amonil officials involved had probably said, "If Gastex won't agree to modify the price term, we won't deliver the by-product," as a way of testing Gastex. Gastex was reportedly nervous about its ability to take delivery on time, and it regarded Amonil's tough talk as a breach of contract. Gastex wanted the contract continued and thought the oil embargo panicked Amonil into abrogating it. Gastex's attorneys thought Amonil could easily live with the contract, which, as it turned out, arguably allowed the price to escalate in mid-1976 when Blatt's Oilgram began reporting prices for new or unreleased oil. Because Gastex felt it probably could never have taken delivery until near the latest date provided in the contract (December 1, 1975), Gastex's attorneys wondered why Amonil didn't simply await developments.

Gastex initiated a line of depositions concerning a point of contract law on which the Gastex-Amonil contract was silent. Could Gastex have engaged in "spot sales" or brokered the by-product it could not use if no conversion plant were ready to receive it? The federal regulations issued in late 1973 were silent or equivocal on this point. Amonil contended that the spirit of the emerging regulatory system would not permit Gastex to spot-sell any unused by-product and that Amonil could not satisfy Gastex as a baseline customer if Gastex was going to act as a broker. Amonil deposed about ten federal officials on this matter, but the Amonil attorneys felt this line of depositions was a "dry hole." Gastex's attorneys, on the other hand, thought the depositions were fruitful for Amonil because they showed a policy of not allowing spot-sale brokerage. From Gastex's perspective, although there was a general policy, federal officials always were careful to say that preexisting contracts were considered on an individual basis, and no spot-sale based on such a contract had ever been disallowed or voided by federal officials.

Amonil conducted another series of depositions of about a dozen Gastex employees. Gastex's attorneys considered these the most grueling of all: the company's president was deposed for nine days concerning Gastex's finances and corporate planning.

Gastex thought Amonil "had been lulled to sleep by being on the offensive for so long" and as the trail of Amonil's depositions petered out, Gastex reopened depositions it had previously taken of Amonil officials, two of whom had since been promoted to high positions within the corporation. Both were deposed on their views of corporation policy toward allocation permits, and their answers conflicted with each other. The higher official said Amonil policy was to execute allocation permits and let the federal government worry about processing the forms further; the other official said no allocation forms were to be executed without prior federal approval. Examination of these officials produced a picture of corporate confusion that Gastex relished.

Gastex's requests to Amonil for price documents had produced an internal memorandum on strategies for dealing with contracts like Gastex's. Three strategies were outlined: the first was renegotiation of the price term, using the recently developed method that Amonil officials brought to the crucial meetings with Gastex for what turned out to be the first time the method was proposed. The second strategy was a Washington lobbying effort to abrogate such contracts through legislation or new regulations. The third was a lobbying effort to persuade Blatt's to change its reporting methods. Although both the plaintiff and the defendant had long used their indexing of documents to prepare successfully for depositions, this memorandum had not been indexed when it was received; Gastex now used it to reopen the depositions of two Amonil officials. The author of the memo was deposed first, and his credibility was reportedly tested by using the document. The testimony gained an admission of authorship, but not of corporate policy, and was used with the memo in the examination of the second official, an Amonil vice-president for sales. Gastex's attorneys thought the most important point of the deposition was the following exchange, in which a Gastex attorney asked the vice-president who had attempted to renegotiate the price term in the agreement:

> Q: Isn't it true that when you started out, you just wanted to renegotiate the term, but upon reflection you decided the contract had ambiguities that needed to be ironed out?
>
> A: Yes, I think that's true.

The question was of the "heads-I-win, tails-you-lose" variety, but the exchange reflected the obscure nature of the contract dispute. Gastex thought itself well on the way to showing a corporate course of conduct amounting to a breach or an anticipatory breach of contract. Thereafter, Gastex increased its resistance to further discovery.

In its responses to Amonil's next set of interrogatories, Gastex said that questions regarding the identity of the preparer of Gastex documents had been answered in the course of seven (named) depositions; the plaintiff further objected to producing these documents again, stating that it had thus far produced about 1,850 documents and expected to produce several hundred more after further searches were completed. Gastex asked for some demonstration of need on other requests and further objected to producing documents not prepared by Gastex employees as irrelevant to the task of contract interpretation necessary to determine which party was in default.

Gastex's answers were deemed unresponsive by Amonil, which filed a motion to compel, particularly regarding Gastex's allegedly incomplete production of documents. Gastex argued, for example, that any motion and order concerning its management committee minutes would be premature, because it was still searching for the minutes. Gastex did not waive any objection to production if the minutes were found, however. Oral requests had been made for the minutes, but Gastex argued that these and similar requests by letter had been rejected as too broad. A week later, in a response to Amonil's third request for production of documents, Gastex's attorneys seemed annoyed: typographical errors in Amonil's papers were noted with "(sic)," and requests for all the stenographic pads of Gastex secretaries--not limited to litigation files--were turned away as too broad, burdensome, or as having already been searched. Gastex raised the same objection to requests for "minutes of meetings" for 1972 to 1974 of four Gastex internal planning committees and records of telephone calls to federal agencies. No documents were found, Gastex reported, in searches for the records of telephone calls to federal agencies, the size of the storage tanks in Gastex's proposed conversion plant, or drafts of the agreement by Gastex's in-house counsel. In deposition, one Gastex employee had said that she kept a "diary" of agreement negotiations for her own use, but that was not located, though Gastex said it was still searching. Gastex did produce preliminary plans and bid specifications for its conversion plant at this time.

Gastex's attorneys asked for a trial date in the hope of ending discovery. In a second status conference, the judge issued a pretrial order and set a trial date four months later, with a discovery cutoff date two months later. Further interrogatories were exchanged to elicit the names of witnesses at trial, and pretrial briefs were filed nineteen months after the filing of the complaint.

For Amonil, the fruits of discovery remained documentary--the highlights were the internal memoranda of Gastex's in-house counsel on interpreting the price term and the exchange of the drafts of the contracts. Amonil's lead attorney reported that he would eliminate one-third of his depositions if he had the case to do over again. Gastex's attorneys, however, conceded that 80 percent of Amonil's depositions were reasonably related to the subject matter of the suit.

What bothered Gastex's attorneys most was the discovery that Amonil had conducted with Blatt's: it lent credence to the theory, reportedly first held by Amonil's in-house trial counsel, that it was Blatt's daily price reporting, not the monthly summaries, to which the contract's price computation referred. The daily reports contained the prices of foreign crude oil long before the Oilgram reported them as a factor influencing domestic oil prices. The method of these daily computations tended to favor Amonil even if the reported monthly prices did not.

Amonil's in-house counsel was in a regional office of the corporation. He responded to any inquiries about out-of-court settlement by saying, "Well, drop the suit." But Amonil's attorneys were hesitant to advise going to trial before a jury composed of Gastex rate payers. Even the judge reported being a Gastex customer. Moreover, the law firm representing Amonil lacked trial experience in this type of litigation, and some of Amonil's in-house counsel wanted to take over the representation if the case went to trial. The Gastex attorneys continued to believe that the issue important to the jury would be the credibility of witnesses who presented conflicting versions of the meetings held in September and October, 1974. Amonil's counsel didn't agree that the issues were limited to facts that could be presented to a jury, and they wanted to limit the jury's role. They felt the case revolved around a question of law, not of fact; they did not concede that any single act constituted a breach of contract. Despite this disagreement over characterization of the issue, Amonil's lawyers respected the skill of Gastex's trial counsel at this type of oral advocacy.

Based on the account of the facts in the briefs, the case apparently remained a relatively narrow contract dispute. Gastex contended that five months before the suit was filed, it provided Amonil with written notice of Amonil's default. Amonil replied to this letter ten days later, saying that it was not in default, but would insist on a new formula for computing the price term. Amonil's contention was that its reformulation was reasonably within the wording of the agreement, which called for using Blatt's Oilgram but did not specify which of three reporting services was to be used. Amonil argued that because Gastex was not going forward with its conversion plant, the plaintiff was not injured, even if (arguendo) Amonil had breached the agreement. Gastex cited memoranda, uncovered in its document search, which showed that Amonil's in-house counsel had advised the corporation on methods to invalidate the agreement six months after its execution and that two months later, Amonil made a policy decision not to deliver the by-product under the agreement.

In its pretrial brief, Amonil argued at length the legal uncertainty of the price term, the parol evidence rule, force majeure (the oil boycott), and several issues involving the measure of damages. Amonil argued that there was no anticipatory breach, but if there was, its reformulated price term in its reply to Gastex's notice of breach cured it. Further, it filed a motion for summary judgment on the plaintiff's "course of conduct" theory. Amonil argued that, as a matter of law, no aggregate of events amounted to an anticipatory breach if no single act was sufficient. It also argued that Gastex must elect either liquidated or consequential damages under the agreement. Amonil listed twenty-one legal questions; Gastex listed two. Amonil still had slightly fewer than a dozen partners working on the case; Gastex had two.

Settlement discussions were initiated during a break in Gastex's depositions of Amonil employees. Gastex offered a form of barter agreement, but Amonil rejected the offer because recent "wildcatting" for oil in new fields had forced it to finance its operations heavily and it "didn't want to barter mortgaged goods." Settlement negotiations were later undertaken by Gastex's in-house counsel directly with Amonil officials, during a week in which Gastex's attorneys were indexing approximately 900 deposition exhibits for trial. The parties settled for a $3 million payment from Amonil to Gastex. The amount represented the value of the contract over the initial five-year period, discounted to its present value at the time of settlement. One of Gastex's attorneys reported that the settlement was paid out of Amonil's petty cash account with a large bank.

www.ingramcontent.com/pod-product-compliance
Lightning Source LLC
Chambersburg PA
CBHW081152180526
45170CB00006B/2041